Kids' Guide to Roller Coasters

Greg Madsen

Chapter 1: What Makes Roller Coasters So Fun?

Introduction to Roller Coasters

Imagine standing in line, hearing the distant roar of a roller coaster as it speeds down a track. The excited screams of riders fill the air as you inch closer to the front. Your heart pounds as you watch the train climb higher and higher, knowing that in just a few moments, you'll be on that very ride, experiencing the thrill for yourself. This is the magic of roller coasters—the rush of excitement, the anticipation, and the unforgettable feeling of soaring through the air at high speeds.

A roller coaster is more than just a ride. It's an experience that combines speed, height, and movement to create an adrenaline rush like no other. Whether it's a towering steel giant with loops and corkscrews or a classic wooden coaster with massive hills and tight turns, these rides have been thrilling people for over a century.

But why do people love them so much? Some riders enjoy the challenge of conquering their fears, while others simply love the feeling of weightlessness and speed. For many, roller coasters are the highlight of a visit to an amusement park, giving them an unforgettable adventure each time they ride.

The Science of Excitement

Why do some people seek out roller coasters while others prefer to stay on the ground? The answer lies in how our brains and bodies react to thrills. When you ride a roller coaster, your body releases three key chemicals:

- **Adrenaline** – This is the "fight-or-flight" hormone that kicks in when you feel excitement or fear. It makes your heart race, your breath quicken, and your muscles tense.
- **Dopamine** – Known as the "feel-good" chemical, dopamine is released when you do something exciting or rewarding. It gives you a sense of pleasure and happiness.
- **Endorphins** – These chemicals help reduce stress and create a sense of euphoria. They're the reason you feel amazing after riding a thrilling roller coaster.

These reactions are part of what makes roller coasters so fun! The combination of excitement, fear, and relief after the ride is over creates a rush that many people love to experience over and over again.

When you ride a roller coaster, your brain is tricked into thinking you're in danger—even though you're completely safe. Your stomach might drop, your arms might tingle, and you might even scream without meaning to! But as soon as the ride ends, your brain realizes that you were never actually in danger, and you're left with a feeling of accomplishment and exhilaration.

Different Types of Thrills

Not all roller coasters provide the same kind of excitement. Some focus on speed, others on height, and some on crazy twists and turns. Here's a look at the different types of thrills you might experience:

- **Fast Coasters:** These rides focus on pure speed, launching riders from zero to over 100 mph in just a few seconds! The rush of acceleration makes it feel like you're being shot out of a cannon. Example: *Formula*

Rossa in Abu Dhabi, the fastest roller coaster in the world at 149 mph.

- **Tall Coasters:** These rides climb to extreme heights, giving riders an amazing view before plunging down at incredible speeds. The anticipation of waiting for the drop is just as thrilling as the fall itself! Example: *Kingda Ka* in New Jersey, which stands at 456 feet tall.
- **Looping Coasters:** These rides feature corkscrews, vertical loops, and other crazy inversions that flip riders upside down. The feeling of twisting through the air is a thrill like no other! Example: *The Smiler* in the UK, which has a world-record 14 inversions.

Each type of coaster offers a unique experience. Some people love the rush of speed, while others enjoy the feeling of flying through loops. Which one sounds the most exciting to you?

What Kind of Coaster Fan Are You?

Not everyone experiences roller coasters the same way. Some kids can't wait to ride the tallest and fastest coasters, while others prefer gentler rides. Which type of coaster rider are you?

- **The Thrill-Seeker** – You love speed, big drops, and the most intense rides. You're always looking for the next big challenge and never say no to a new coaster.
- **The Casual Rider** – You enjoy roller coasters, but you're not in a rush to ride the scariest ones. You might prefer smooth rides without too many loops or extreme drops.
- **The Nervous First-Timer** – You're curious about roller coasters, but they make you a little nervous. You might stick to smaller rides until you feel ready for the big ones.

If you're a first-time rider, don't worry! Many people feel nervous before their first big roller coaster ride. The good news is that there are ways to build confidence:

- Start with smaller coasters and work your way up to bigger ones.
- Ride with a friend or family member who enjoys coasters.
- Watch a POV (point-of-view) video online so you know what to expect.
- Remember that roller coasters are designed to be safe and fun!

No matter what type of coaster fan you are, there's a ride out there for you.

Memorable First Rides

Everyone remembers their first roller coaster ride. It's a mix of excitement, nervousness, and anticipation. Here are a few stories from kids who rode their first coasters:

- **Liam, Age 10:** "I was really scared to go on my first big coaster, but my dad convinced me to try it. When we went down the first drop, I screamed so loud, but by the end, I wanted to go again!"
- **Emma, Age 9:** "I rode my first looping coaster at Disney World, and I was so nervous about going upside down. But it was so smooth and fun, I laughed the whole time!"
- **Jacob, Age 11:** "My first roller coaster had a launch instead of a chain lift, so we went from zero to 70 mph in seconds. It felt like a rocket ship!"

If you haven't been on a roller coaster yet, how should you prepare for your first big ride?

- Pick a coaster that's exciting but not too intense for your first time.
- Try sitting in the middle of the train (the front feels the fastest, and the back has the biggest drops).
- Keep your hands on the lap bar and take deep breaths before the ride starts.
- Remember, the first drop is usually the scariest part—after that, it's just fun!

Your first roller coaster ride is an experience you'll never forget. Whether you're laughing, screaming, or closing your eyes, it's a moment that will make you want to come back for more.

Bringing It All Together

Roller coasters are one of the most exciting attractions at amusement parks. They make us scream, laugh, and feel a rush like no other ride. Whether you love high-speed launches, towering drops, or twisting loops, there's a coaster out there for you.

From the thrill of waiting in line to the rush of the first drop, roller coasters bring a mix of emotions that keep riders coming back again and again. Whether you're a thrill-seeker or just getting started, the world of roller coasters is full of exciting rides and unforgettable memories.

So, are you ready to take on your next coaster adventure? Buckle up, hold on tight, and get ready for the ride of a lifetime!

Chapter 2: A Ride Through History

Where It All Began

Before roller coasters had loops, steep drops, or lightning-fast speeds, thrill-seekers had to find excitement in much simpler ways. Believe it or not, the origins of roller coasters can be traced back to the **1600s in Russia**, where people enjoyed sliding down massive ice-covered hills on wooden sleds. These rides, known as *Russian Mountains*, were built using stacked layers of ice, and riders would sit on blocks of wood with straw padding for cushioning. While these early rides were slow compared to modern roller coasters, they were incredibly popular and became a favorite pastime during the cold Russian winters.

As time went on, people began looking for ways to improve the experience. By the **late 1700s**, French inventors took the idea of the Russian ice slides and added **wheeled carts** that ran on wooden tracks. This was the first major step toward what we now recognize as roller coasters. These rides, called *Les Montagnes Russes* (which means "Russian Mountains" in French), were the earliest versions of what would become the thrilling coasters we know today.

One of the first roller coaster-like attractions was built in **1817 in Paris**, called the *Promenades Aériennes* (Aerial Walks). This ride had guided cars that followed a track with gentle hills and curves, giving riders a smoother and more controlled experience. Over time, these attractions grew more exciting, leading to a new kind of thrill ride.

The First Official Roller Coaster

Fast forward to **1884**, when the first true roller coaster was introduced in the United States. Called the **Gravity Pleasure**

Switchback Railway, this historic ride was built at **Coney Island in Brooklyn, New York**, by a man named **LaMarcus Adna Thompson**. Unlike modern roller coasters, this ride was much simpler—it consisted of a small train that coasted down a wooden track from one tower to another, reaching speeds of about **6 miles per hour**.

Even though it wasn't very fast, it was incredibly popular. People loved the feeling of gliding down the track, and within weeks, the ride was making **over $600 per day**—a huge success at the time. The *Switchback Railway* quickly became a blueprint for future roller coasters. Soon, amusement parks across the country were building their own versions, improving the design to make them **longer, taller, and more thrilling**.

Thompson is often credited as the *father of the modern roller coaster*, as he continued developing new ride ideas, including **dark tunnel coasters** that added an extra element of surprise. Thanks to his innovations, roller coasters quickly became one of the most popular attractions at amusement parks.

Early Wooden Coasters

By the early **1900s**, amusement parks were booming, and wooden roller coasters became the stars of the show. These coasters had:

- **Massive wooden structures** that supported steep hills and drops.
- **Chain lifts** to pull the cars up to the top of the first hill.
- **Gravity-powered trains** that coasted along the track using momentum.

One of the earliest and most famous wooden coasters was **The Scenic Railway**, built in **1912** in Melbourne, Australia. Unlike today's coasters, this ride actually required a **brakeman** to ride along with the train and manually slow it down when needed!

The thrill of wooden coasters came from their **bumpy, rattling ride experience**. Even though they didn't have loops or extreme speeds, their tall drops and sharp turns made them exciting. Some of these classic wooden coasters are still in operation today, proving that a great roller coaster doesn't need to be high-tech to be fun!

The Golden Age of Coasters (1920s-1930s)

The **1920s and 1930s** were known as the **Golden Age of Roller Coasters**. During this time, amusement parks were growing in popularity, and coaster designers were **pushing the limits** of what was possible.

- **New coaster designs** introduced steeper drops, tighter turns, and thrilling speeds.
- **Bigger and better parks** opened across the U.S., including **Luna Park, Riverview Park, and Kennywood**.
- **Record-breaking coasters** such as the *Cyclone* at Coney Island (built in 1927) became legendary rides.

One of the most famous coasters from this era was the **Crystal Beach Cyclone**, which was so intense that **some riders fainted from the extreme forces**! Even though many of these early wooden coasters no longer exist, their designs inspired the rides that followed.

Unfortunately, by the **1940s**, the Great Depression and World War II caused amusement parks to struggle, leading to many roller coasters being shut down or dismantled. The future of coasters seemed uncertain—until the **1950s**, when a new kind of technology changed everything.

The Steel Revolution (1950s-Present)

The biggest turning point in roller coaster history came in the **1950s**, when designers invented a **new kind of track—tubular steel rails**. Unlike wooden coasters, which had **flat tracks**, these new steel rails allowed for **smoother, faster, and more complex rides**.

The first modern **steel roller coaster**, called the **Matterhorn Bobsleds**, was built at **Disneyland in 1959**. It was the first coaster to:

- Use **tubular steel tracks** for a smoother ride.
- Feature a **mountain theme**, making it part of a larger park experience.
- Have a **fully enclosed structure**, creating a ride-through adventure.

Steel tracks allowed designers to create **loops, corkscrews, and twisting inversions** that wouldn't have been possible with wooden coasters. This led to **inverted coasters, suspended coasters, and launch coasters**, which made roller coasters more exciting than ever before.

By the **1970s and 1980s, parks like Six Flags and Cedar Point** were competing to build the tallest, fastest, and most intense rides. Roller coaster technology was advancing rapidly, and each new ride was bigger and better than the last.

Modern-Day Roller Coasters

Today, roller coasters have reached **incredible heights and speeds**. Some of the most **mind-blowing coasters** in the world include:

- **Kingda Ka (USA)** – The tallest coaster in the world at **456 feet**!
- **Formula Rossa (UAE)** – The fastest coaster, reaching **149 mph** in just a few seconds.
- **Steel Vengeance (USA)** – A record-breaking hybrid coaster combining **wood and steel**.
- **The Smiler (UK)** – The ride with the most loops—**14 inversions**!

Modern roller coasters continue to push the limits with:

- **Magnetic launch systems** instead of traditional chain lifts.
- **Hybrid coasters** that combine wooden structures with steel tracks.
- **Virtual reality experiences**, where riders wear VR headsets for an added layer of excitement.

With new rides being designed every year, the future of roller coasters looks brighter than ever. Who knows what the next big innovation will be? **Could we see underwater coasters, flying coasters, or even roller coasters in space?**

One thing is for sure: roller coasters will continue to excite, thrill, and entertain people for generations to come. Whether you love the classic wooden rides or the latest steel giants, there's a perfect roller coaster for everyone!

Chapter 3: Famous Roller Coasters Around the World

Record-Breaking Coasters

Roller coasters are always evolving, and parks around the world constantly compete to build the biggest, fastest, and most extreme rides. Some coasters hold records for their height, speed, or length, making them must-ride attractions for thrill-seekers.

- **Tallest Coaster in the World: Kingda Ka (USA)**

  - Located at Six Flags Great Adventure in New Jersey, *Kingda Ka* towers at **456 feet**, making it the tallest roller coaster on Earth.
  - It launches riders from **0 to 128 mph in just 3.5 seconds**, sending them straight up before plummeting down a heart-stopping drop.
  - The height alone is enough to scare some people away, but for coaster enthusiasts, it's a bucket-list ride.
- **Fastest Coaster in the World: Formula Rossa (UAE)**

  - Found at Ferrari World in Abu Dhabi, *Formula Rossa* reaches an **incredible speed of 149 mph**, making it the fastest roller coaster on the planet.
  - The ride is so fast that riders must wear **goggles** to protect their eyes from the wind and sand!
- **Longest Coaster in the World: Steel Dragon 2000 (Japan)**

  - Located at Nagashima Spa Land, *Steel Dragon 2000* holds the record for the **longest track length**, stretching over **8,133 feet** (more than 1.5 miles).
  - The ride lasts over **four minutes**, making it one of the most endurance-testing roller coasters in existence.
- **Steepest Drop in the World: TMNT Shellraiser (USA)**

  - At Nickelodeon Universe in New Jersey, *TMNT Shellraiser* holds the record for the **steepest**

drop, at **121.5 degrees**—meaning the drop actually angles inward!

- This beyond-vertical drop creates the feeling of free-falling forward before leveling out.

Each year, new rides break old records, with designers finding innovative ways to push the limits. With taller, faster, and steeper coasters being introduced, one thing is clear: the roller coaster wars are far from over!

Classic Roller Coasters

Even though record-breaking coasters steal the spotlight, some of the most beloved roller coasters are the ones that have stood the test of time. These classic rides may not be the tallest or fastest, but they remain legendary for their history, charm, and thrilling ride experiences.

- **Leap-the-Dips (USA, 1902)**

  - Located at Lakemont Park in Pennsylvania, *Leap-the-Dips* is the **oldest operating roller coaster in the world.**
  - This wooden coaster, built in **1902**, has no seat belts or lap bars—just a simple track and gravity keeping riders in place!
  - It may not be as extreme as modern rides, but its historical significance makes it a must-ride for coaster fans.

- **The Cyclone (USA, 1927)**

  - One of the most famous wooden coasters ever built, *The Cyclone* at Coney Island is still thrilling riders nearly **100 years** after it first opened.

- o Its aggressive turns and airtime hills make it one of the most intense wooden coasters in the world.
- **Grand National (UK, 1935)**

  - o Found at Blackpool Pleasure Beach in England, *Grand National* is a rare **racing wooden coaster**, meaning two trains run side by side as they race to the finish.
  - o This classic coaster is beloved for its unique design and old-school thrills.

Wooden coasters may not have the loops and smoothness of modern steel coasters, but their history and character make them special. The feeling of the track shaking beneath you, the sound of the wooden beams creaking, and the classic out-of-control sensation keep these coasters popular generation after generation.

The Most Themed Coasters

While some coasters focus on pure thrills, others use **storytelling and special effects** to create an immersive experience. These themed coasters transport riders into different worlds, combining excitement with detailed environments, music, and animatronics.

- **Space Mountain (Disney Parks)**

  - o Found in Disney theme parks around the world, *Space Mountain* is a **dark indoor roller coaster** that makes riders feel like they're flying through outer space.
  - o The ride's **music, lighting effects, and star projections** make it feel faster than it actually is.

- **The VelociCoaster (USA)**

  - Universal's *VelociCoaster* at Islands of Adventure (Florida) combines a high-speed launch coaster with an immersive **Jurassic World** theme.
  - Before even getting on the ride, guests walk through **realistic dinosaur enclosures** with animatronic raptors.
  - The ride itself features **two launches, four inversions, and a 140-foot-tall top hat element**, making it one of the best thrill rides in the world.
- **Expedition Everest (USA)**

  - Another Disney masterpiece, *Expedition Everest* at Animal Kingdom features a **mystical Himalayan adventure**, complete with a **giant animatronic Yeti** that "attacks" riders mid-ride.
  - The coaster even includes **a surprise backward section**, making it unique among Disney rides.

These coasters prove that a ride isn't just about speed and drops—it's about **creating an experience**. Theming makes rides more memorable, turning them into **full-blown adventures**.

Roller Coasters by Country

While the U.S. is home to some of the most famous coasters, other countries have their own incredible rides. Here's a look at some of the best coasters from around the world:

- **United States:** Known for the most **record-breaking coasters**, including *Kingda Ka, Steel Vengeance,* and *Millennium Force.*
- **Japan:** Home to unique and intense rides like *Eejanaika* (a **4D spinning coaster**) and *Takabisha* (the **world's steepest coaster**).
- **Germany:** Famous for **smooth, well-engineered rides**, including *Silver Star* (one of Europe's tallest coasters) and *Taron* (a multi-launch masterpiece).
- **United Kingdom:** Home to *The Smiler*, the coaster with the **most inversions in the world** (14 loops!).
- **United Arab Emirates:** Known for extreme speed, with *Formula Rossa* holding the record for **fastest coaster on Earth**.

Each country has its own style of coasters, influenced by different cultural preferences and engineering techniques.

Would You Ride These?

Some roller coasters push the boundaries of what's possible, making even the bravest riders think twice before getting on. Here are a few of the **most extreme and unusual coasters** in the world:

- **Takabisha (Japan)** – The world's **steepest coaster**, with a terrifying **121.5-degree drop**.
- **X2 (USA)** – A **4D coaster** where seats rotate **independently** of the track, flipping riders head-over-heels.
- **SkyCycle (Japan)** – Instead of being powered by gravity, riders **pedal their own coaster carts** along a narrow track high above the ground!
- **Gravity Max (Taiwan)** – The world's only **tilt coaster**, where the track suddenly **stops, tilts forward 90 degrees, and drops riders straight down**.

- **Eejanaika (Japan)** – One of the most extreme roller coasters ever, where riders flip head-over-heels **14 times** while traveling at breakneck speeds.

These rides take thrills to the next level, offering experiences unlike anything else. Would you dare to ride them?

Bringing It All Together

Roller coasters come in all shapes, sizes, and levels of intensity. From **record-breaking giants** to **classic wooden rides**, from **themed adventures** to **outrageously extreme coasters**, the world is full of exciting rides waiting to be experienced.

Whether you prefer **speed, height, inversions, or immersive storytelling**, there's a roller coaster out there for everyone. With new coasters being built every year, the future of these thrilling rides is more exciting than ever!

So, which famous roller coaster would you want to ride first?

Chapter 4: How Roller Coasters Work

The Science Behind the Thrill

Roller coasters may seem like magic, but they actually operate based on **scientific principles** that have been around for centuries. Every twist, turn, and drop is designed to use **energy and motion** in a way that creates thrills while keeping riders safe.

At the heart of a roller coaster's movement are **potential energy and kinetic energy**:

- **Potential Energy** is stored energy. When a roller coaster is at the top of its first big hill, it has the most potential energy because gravity is waiting to pull it downward.
- **Kinetic Energy** is energy in motion. When the coaster drops from the top, potential energy is converted into kinetic energy, which gives the ride its speed.

This is why the **first hill** on a traditional roller coaster is usually the tallest—because it needs to build up enough potential energy to carry the train through the entire ride. Once it gains speed from that first drop, the ride relies on momentum and gravity to keep it going.

But what about **launch coasters** that don't have a big first hill? These use powerful **mechanical systems** (like magnets or hydraulics) to give the train a burst of speed, generating kinetic energy right away. Whether it's a towering hill or a launch track, the goal is the same: create enough energy to power the coaster through the course.

Gravity and Momentum

One of the most fascinating things about roller coasters is that **they don't need engines** to keep them moving after the first drop. Instead, they rely entirely on **gravity and momentum** to carry them along the track.

- **Gravity** pulls the coaster downward when it reaches the top of a hill, causing it to accelerate.
- **Momentum** (the force that keeps objects moving) helps the train coast through loops, turns, and airtime hills.

If you've ever noticed that some coaster hills get **smaller as the ride continues**, that's because the train is slowly losing energy due to **friction** (resistance from the air and track). Engineers design coasters carefully so they don't slow down too soon—every hill and curve is placed **precisely** to ensure a smooth ride from start to finish.

But how do coasters **stay on the track**, even when going upside down? That's where **centripetal force** comes in. When a coaster enters a loop, it's moving so fast that the force of motion pushes riders **into their seats** rather than letting them fall. This is the same force that keeps water inside a bucket if you swing it in a circle.

By carefully balancing **gravity, momentum, and centripetal force**, designers ensure that roller coasters feel fast and thrilling without flying off the track!

The Anatomy of a Roller Coaster

A roller coaster is more than just a train on a track—it's a complex machine made up of several important parts:

- **The Track** – The rails that guide the coaster train. Tracks can be made of wood or steel, with steel allowing for **loops and smoother rides**.

- **The Trains** – The cars that carry riders. Some have **open seats for maximum exposure**, while others have **enclosed capsules** for added safety.
- **The Supports** – The structure that holds the track in place. On **wooden coasters**, this looks like a lattice of beams, while steel coasters often have **thinner, taller supports**.
- **The Wheels** – Coasters have three types of wheels to keep them safely on the track:
    - **Running Wheels** (on top of the track) – Control the train's movement.
    - **Side Wheels** (on the sides of the track) – Prevent side-to-side movement.
    - **Underfriction Wheels** (beneath the track) – Keep the train from lifting off.

These components work together to make sure coasters **stay on course**, delivering an exciting but controlled experience.

How Coasters Are Launched

Not all roller coasters start with a slow climb up a hill. Some use **advanced launch systems** to propel riders at incredible speeds in just seconds.

1. **Chain Lift (Traditional Method)**

    - This is the classic way roller coasters begin. A large metal chain pulls the train **up the first hill**, using a motorized pulley system.
    - Once the train reaches the top, gravity takes over, and the rest of the ride is powered by momentum.
    - Example: *The Beast* (Kings Island) uses a traditional chain lift to pull riders up a **137-foot hill** before sending them into the woods.

2. **Hydraulic Launch (Extreme Acceleration)**

   - Hydraulic launch systems use **pressurized fluid and cables** to create an incredibly fast takeoff.
   - These launches can send coasters from **0 to 128 mph in just a few seconds!**
   - Example: *Kingda Ka* (Six Flags Great Adventure) uses **hydraulic launch technology** to catapult riders **straight up a 456-foot hill** in 3.5 seconds.

3. **Magnetic Launch (Modern Innovation)**

   - Many new coasters use **magnetic launch systems (LSM or LIM)** to smoothly accelerate trains without the need for a chain or hydraulics.
   - These magnets **push and pull** the train along the track, offering a quieter and more energy-efficient ride.
   - Example: *VelociCoaster* (Universal Orlando) uses **two magnetic launches**, one of which accelerates riders **to 70 mph mid-ride**.

Launch coasters provide a different kind of thrill than traditional chain lifts. Instead of **building suspense** with a slow climb, they **shock riders** with an instant burst of speed!

How Brakes Work

Every thrilling ride has to come to an end—but how do roller coasters slow down smoothly without **slamming on the brakes**? Coasters use **carefully designed braking systems** to stop the train safely and comfortably.

1. **Friction Brakes (Traditional Brakes)**

- These are like the brakes on a car, using **pads that press against the train's wheels** to create friction and slow it down.
- Friction brakes are often found **at the end of a ride**, gradually bringing the train to a stop.

2. **Magnetic Brakes (Modern Coasters)**

- Many modern coasters use **magnets** instead of friction to slow the train.
- Magnets provide a **smoother stop** and don't wear down like traditional brakes.
- Example: *Intimidator 305* (Kings Dominion) slows down with magnetic brakes after its **305-foot drop**.

3. **Trim Brakes (Mid-Ride Speed Control)**

- Some coasters have **trim brakes** in the middle of the ride to **adjust speed**.
- This prevents trains from going too fast around turns or through loops.
- Example: *Millennium Force* (Cedar Point) has trim brakes on one of its hills to **ensure a comfortable speed**.

Thanks to these braking systems, roller coasters can deliver **fast, intense rides** while ensuring a smooth, controlled stop.

Mastering the Mechanics of Coasters

Roller coasters may seem like simple thrill machines, but they're actually built on **precise science and engineering**. Every loop, drop, and turn is carefully designed to balance **speed, gravity, and safety**.

From the moment a train **climbs its first hill or launches forward**, forces like **kinetic energy, momentum, and centripetal force** keep it moving. The **track, wheels, and braking systems** ensure that riders experience thrills while staying completely secure.

Whether you're riding a **classic chain-lift coaster** or a **high-speed launch coaster**, the magic of roller coasters comes from their perfect mix of **science and excitement**. So, next time you buckle into a coaster, think about all the forces at work—then, hold on tight and enjoy the ride!

Chapter 5: Types of Roller Coasters

Wooden vs. Steel Coasters

One of the first things people notice about roller coasters is whether they're made of **wood or steel**. These two materials create completely different ride experiences, each with its own set of thrills.

- **Wooden Coasters**

  - **Built using thick wooden beams** with metal tracks running along the top.
  - Tend to have **bumpier, rougher rides**, which some people love for their classic feel.
  - Often feature **big hills and fast turns** but **no loops** due to the rigid structure.
  - Example: *The Beast* at Kings Island, one of the longest and most famous wooden coasters.
- **Steel Coasters**

  - Made from **smooth tubular steel** that allows for **loops, corkscrews, and crazy turns**.
  - Provide a **smoother and faster ride**, making them more comfortable for many riders.
  - Come in a wider variety of shapes and styles, including inverted and launch coasters.
  - Example: *Millennium Force* at Cedar Point, a record-breaking steel coaster known for its speed.

Pros and Cons of Each Type

Feature	Wooden Coasters	Steel Coasters

Smoothness	Rougher ride, more bumpy	Very smooth, less shaking
Speed	Can be fast but limited	Much faster with higher top speeds
Loops/Inversions	Usually none	Many loops, corkscrews, and twists
Durability	Requires more maintenance	Longer-lasting with fewer repairs
Thrill Factor	Classic "out-of-control" feel	High-speed excitement and steep drops

Both types have their fans—some people love the **classic, rickety charm** of wooden coasters, while others prefer the **high-tech thrills** of steel coasters.

Traditional Coaster Types

Before roller coasters had extreme designs with **loops and launches**, they followed a few classic layouts. These traditional coaster types can still be found in many amusement parks today.

- **Out-and-Back Coasters**

  - A simple **"U-shaped" track** with big hills in a straight line before returning to the station.
  - These coasters focus on **airtime**, where riders lift off their seats on the drops.
  - Example: *Phoenix* (Knoebels), one of the most famous out-and-back coasters.
- **Twister Coasters**

  - Instead of a straight layout, these coasters **twist and turn in all directions**.
  - They feel more **intense** because riders don't know what's coming next.
  - Example: *The Cyclone* (Coney Island), a legendary wooden twister coaster.
- **Wild Mouse Coasters**

  - Known for their **sharp turns and small, jerky movements**.
  - Have **individual cars instead of long trains**, making each turn feel even tighter.
  - Example: *Matterhorn Bobsleds* (Disneyland), a classic Wild Mouse-style coaster.

These coaster styles set the foundation for today's more advanced designs.

Modern Coaster Types

Thanks to engineering advancements, roller coasters have evolved far beyond the classic designs. Here are some of the most popular modern coaster types:

- **Inverted Coasters**

    - Instead of sitting **on top of the track**, riders hang **below it**, with their feet dangling.
    - These coasters are known for **smooth loops and fast twists**.
    - Example: *Montu* (Busch Gardens Tampa), one of the most famous inverted coasters.
- **Floorless Coasters**

    - Similar to inverted coasters, but riders sit **above the track**—just with **no floor beneath their feet!**
    - This creates the illusion of **floating in mid-air** while zooming through loops.
    - Example: *Kraken* (SeaWorld Orlando).
- **Giga and Hyper Coasters**

    - **Hyper coasters** are **200-299 feet tall**, focusing on speed and airtime.
    - **Giga coasters** take it even further, standing **300-399 feet tall!**
    - These coasters focus more on **height and speed** than loops.
    - Example: *Millennium Force* (Cedar Point), one of the world's first giga coasters.

Modern coaster designs allow for **bigger and wilder experiences** while keeping rides smooth and safe.

Special Coaster Designs

Beyond traditional and modern coaster types, some coasters take creativity to the next level. These unique designs make rides even more immersive and unpredictable.

- **Flying Coasters**

    - Riders are tilted **face-down**, making them feel like they're **soaring through the air**.
    - Example: *Tatsu* (Six Flags Magic Mountain), which gives the sensation of flying over mountains.
- **Spinning Coasters**

    - The **seats spin freely** as the train moves, meaning **every ride is different!**
    - Example: *Time Traveler* (Silver Dollar City), which features both **spinning cars and inversions**.
- **4D Coasters**

    - One of the **craziest coaster types**, where the **seats flip and rotate independently** of the track.
    - Riders experience constant unexpected movements.
    - Example: *X2* (Six Flags Magic Mountain), the first-ever 4D coaster.

These coaster designs add new dimensions to the traditional ride experience, making them some of the most sought-after attractions in the world.

The Future of Coaster Types

What's next for roller coasters? Engineers are constantly **pushing the limits** to create even more thrilling and unique rides. Here are some predictions for the future of roller coasters:

- **AI-Controlled Coasters**

  - Imagine a ride that **adjusts its speed and elements** in real time based on how riders react.
  - Future coasters may use **artificial intelligence** to customize each ride experience.
- **Energy-Efficient Rides**

  - New coasters are being designed to use **less energy** by harnessing **solar power and regenerative braking**.
  - Parks are looking for ways to make thrill rides more environmentally friendly.
- **Water Coaster Hybrids**

  - Future coasters might **combine traditional tracks with water elements**, creating **fully immersive experiences**.
  - Imagine a ride that launches into the air **before plunging into a splash-filled finale!**
- **Holographic and Augmented Reality Coasters**

  - Some coasters already use **virtual reality headsets**, but in the future, we might see **holographic projections** that blend real and digital elements.
  - Riders could **see creatures, special effects, or even interact with the ride in new ways**.

The next 20 years will bring some of the **wildest coaster experiences yet**—perhaps even rides that **defy gravity or move in completely new ways**!

A World of Endless Thrills

Roller coasters come in **all shapes, sizes, and styles**, each offering a unique thrill. From **classic wooden coasters** to **high-tech 4D rides**, there's a roller coaster for **every kind of rider**.

- Some coasters focus on **pure speed and height**.
- Others create **an illusion of flying** or **make riders spin unpredictably**.
- And in the future, **AI-powered, eco-friendly, and interactive rides** could change the way we experience roller coasters forever.

No matter how much technology advances, one thing is certain—**roller coasters will always be about thrills, excitement, and unforgettable experiences**. So, which type of coaster do you want to ride next?

Chapter 6: Loops, Drops, and Speeds

Why Roller Coasters Have Drops and Loops

Every great roller coaster has a moment where riders **hold their breath in anticipation**—whether it's at the top of a towering drop or as the train flips upside down in a massive loop. Drops and inversions (loops, corkscrews, and rolls) are two of the biggest thrills on a roller coaster, and they rely on both **science and engineering** to make them exciting and safe.

- **The Role of Height in Speed**

    - The taller a roller coaster, the more **potential energy** it builds up before the first drop.
    - As the train starts descending, that potential energy **converts into kinetic energy**, making the coaster go faster.
    - That's why roller coasters often start with a **huge lift hill or a powerful launch**—they need to store enough energy to keep the train moving throughout the ride.
- **Why the First Drop Is Usually the Tallest**

    - Many roller coasters have their **biggest drop right at the start** because that's when they have the most energy.
    - After the first drop, the coaster slows down slightly as it moves through turns, loops, and smaller hills.
    - Some coasters, like *Hyperion* in Poland, include a **second huge drop** mid-ride to keep the excitement going.
- **Loops, Corkscrews, and Inversions**

- Loops and inversions create the **thrill of being upside down** while keeping riders completely safe.
- The key to making loops enjoyable (and not painful) is **centripetal force**, which pushes riders into their seats rather than making them feel like they're falling.
- Different types of inversions—like **corkscrews and zero-G rolls**—add variety to the ride experience.

Without drops and loops, roller coasters wouldn't be nearly as exciting. They are carefully designed to provide the **perfect balance of fear and fun** while using physics to keep riders secure.

The Science of Going Fast

Speed is one of the **biggest factors** that makes a roller coaster thrilling. Whether it's a traditional drop or a **high-speed launch**, the goal is to create **intense acceleration** that makes riders feel like they're flying.

- **How Gravity Builds Speed**

  - Gravity is the main **force that makes roller coasters move**.
  - When a coaster reaches the top of a hill, it has built-up **potential energy**—and when it drops, gravity takes over and turns that energy into speed.
  - The steeper the drop, the **faster the train falls** and the more energy it gains for the rest of the ride.
- **The Fastest Roller Coasters in the World**

- *Formula Rossa* (Ferrari World, UAE) – **149 mph**, using a **hydraulic launch system**.
- *Kingda Ka* (Six Flags Great Adventure, USA) – **128 mph**, reaching its speed in just **3.5 seconds**.
- *Red Force* (Ferrari Land, Spain) – **112 mph**, with a vertical launch up a **367-foot tower**.

These coasters don't just rely on drops—they use **launch systems** powered by magnets or hydraulics to blast riders forward at extreme speeds.

The Steepest Drops Ever

Roller coaster drops come in all shapes and sizes, but some of the most **jaw-dropping** rides feature **near-vertical or even beyond-vertical** drops that make riders feel like they're falling straight down.

- **The Fear Factor of Steep Drops**

  - A **90-degree drop** creates a true free-fall sensation, where riders feel **weightless** as they plummet.
  - Some coasters go even steeper than 90 degrees, tilting inward to create the **illusion of falling past vertical**.
- **Coasters with the Steepest Drops**

  - *TMNT Shellraiser* (USA) – **121.5 degrees**, the steepest drop in the world.
  - *Takabisha* (Japan) – **121 degrees**, a beyond-vertical drop combined with **multiple inversions**.
  - *Cannibal* (USA) – **116 degrees**, featuring an enclosed elevator lift before the insane drop.

- **How Designers Make Steep Drops Safe**

  - Even though these drops feel terrifying, **track curvature and braking systems** are carefully engineered to slow down the train at the right moments.
  - Restraints, such as **lap bars or over-the-shoulder harnesses**, hold riders securely so they feel safe even during extreme drops.

Steep drops add a **dramatic, heart-pounding moment** to the start of a ride, making them some of the most **talked-about** elements of any roller coaster.

The Art of Designing a Loop

Loops are one of the most **exciting elements** of a roller coaster, but they're also one of the most scientifically complex. If you've ever wondered how you can go **upside down without falling out**, it all comes down to **physics and careful design**.

- **Why Loops Are Not Perfect Circles**

  - Early roller coasters tried to make loops **circular**, but these caused painful g-forces.
  - Modern loops are shaped like **a teardrop**, which is called a **clothoid loop**.
  - This shape keeps **g-forces more balanced**, so riders don't feel too much pressure on their bodies.
- **How You Stay in Your Seat While Upside Down**

  - When a coaster enters a loop, it's moving so fast that **centripetal force** pushes riders **into their seats**.

- Even if the train didn't have restraints, **you wouldn't fall out** because of how the forces work.
- **Different Types of Inversions**

  - **Vertical Loop** – A standard loop, like on *Superman: Escape from Krypton*.
  - **Corkscrew** – A slow, twisting inversion.
  - **Zero-G Roll** – A roll that makes riders feel weightless for a second.
  - **Cobra Roll** – A double-inversion that flips riders twice.

Each inversion creates a **different sensation**, from **smooth and floaty to quick and intense**.

Comparing Different Types of Drops and Inversions

Not all drops and loops feel the same! Here's how different coaster elements create **unique ride experiences**:

- **Airtime Hills vs. Straight Drops**

  - **Airtime hills** create the feeling of **floating out of your seat** (negative G-forces).
  - **Straight drops** provide a sudden rush of acceleration, making riders feel like they're falling straight down.
- **Different Types of Inversions**

  - **Barrel Roll** – A slow roll that gives a **smooth twisting motion**.
  - **Zero-G Stall** – A pause mid-loop that makes riders feel **completely weightless**.
  - **Cobra Roll** – A double inversion that flips riders twice in a row.

Each of these elements **adds variety to a coaster**, making the ride experience unpredictable and thrilling.

Thrill Engineering: What Makes a Ride Exciting?

Roller coaster loops, drops, and speeds are carefully designed to give riders **just the right mix of fear and excitement**. Whether it's the **free-fall sensation of a steep drop** or the **sensation of weightlessness in a loop**, these elements work together to create a **memorable ride experience**.

- **Tall first drops build speed and momentum.**
- **Steep drops give the feeling of free-fall.**
- **Loops and inversions use physics to make upside-down moments thrilling but safe.**
- **Different coaster elements create different types of excitement.**

The next time you ride a roller coaster, pay attention to how the **drops, loops, and speeds** work together—because every element is **designed to give you the ultimate thrill ride!**

Chapter 7: The Role of Gravity and G-Forces

What Are G-Forces?

If you've ever ridden a roller coaster and felt like you were **glued to your seat** one moment and **floating in mid-air** the next, you've experienced **G-forces**. These invisible forces are what make roller coasters feel thrilling.

G-force (gravitational force) is the measurement of **acceleration relative to gravity**. On Earth, we experience **1G** at all times because that's the normal pull of gravity keeping us on the ground. But roller coasters can **increase or decrease G-forces**, creating some of the most exciting sensations on a ride.

Astronauts, fighter pilots, and race car drivers also experience extreme G-forces:

- **Astronauts** feel **up to 3G or more** during launch, meaning their bodies feel **three times heavier than normal**.
- **Fighter pilots** can experience **up to 9G**, which can cause **blackouts** if the body can't handle the pressure.
- **Roller coaster riders** typically experience anywhere from **-1G to 6G**, depending on the ride's design.

The key to a fun roller coaster ride is using G-forces in a way that creates **excitement without causing discomfort**.

Positive vs. Negative Gs

There are three main types of **G-forces** that affect roller coaster riders:

- **Positive Gs (When You Feel Heavy)**

  - Occur when a coaster pushes riders into their seats.
  - Riders feel **heavier than normal**, like their bodies are being pressed down.
  - Example: When going through the **bottom of a loop** or a **high-speed turn**.
  - Some rides can reach **5G or more**, meaning riders feel **five times heavier** than normal.
- **Negative Gs (When You Feel Weightless)**

  - Occur when riders **lift out of their seats**, creating a feeling of floating.
  - Known as **"airtime"**, negative Gs make riders feel like they're **being pulled out of the coaster car**.
  - Example: When going **over the top of a hill** or on a ride with sharp **airtime bumps**.
  - Some coasters, like *El Toro* and *Steel Vengeance*, are famous for their **intense airtime moments**.
- **Lateral Gs (Sideways Forces)**

  - Happen during **sharp turns** or unexpected **twists**.
  - Instead of being pushed **up or down**, riders are pushed **sideways**.
  - Example: On **wild mouse coasters**, where cars make sudden left or right turns.
  - Banked turns help control lateral Gs, so riders don't slide around too much.

Each type of G-force plays a role in making **roller coasters exciting, unpredictable, and thrilling**.

How Roller Coasters Use G-Forces to Feel Thrilling

Every twist, turn, and drop on a roller coaster is carefully designed to **control G-forces** and create different sensations.

- **Weightless Moments (Zero-G)**

    - Some roller coasters create moments of **zero gravity**, where riders experience a feeling of complete **weightlessness**.
    - Example: Zero-G rolls and stalls, like on *VelociCoaster* and *Twisted Colossus*.
    - These elements make riders feel like they're **floating in space**.
- **Balancing Excitement and Safety**

    - While G-forces make roller coasters fun, they must be **carefully controlled** to avoid making riders uncomfortable.
    - Too many **positive Gs** can make a ride feel **too intense**, while too many **negative Gs** can be dangerous if restraints aren't tight enough.
    - Engineers **test different ride layouts** to find the perfect balance.

Coaster designers **combine different G-forces** to keep riders **on the edge of their seats**—literally!

The Strongest G-Forces on Any Ride

Some roller coasters are famous for their **insane G-forces**, giving riders an **extreme thrill**.

- **The Roller Coaster with the Highest G-Forces: Tower of Terror (South Africa)**

- Pulls **6.3G** at its most intense moment, making it one of the strongest coasters ever built.
- For comparison, astronauts experience about **3G** during a rocket launch!
- **The Most Intense Looping Coaster: G-Force (UK)**

  - Featured a **tight inversion** that reached over **4G** at its peak.
- **The Fastest Coaster: Formula Rossa (UAE)**

  - Reaches **149 mph in 4.9 seconds**, producing **intense G-forces** on the initial launch.
- **Coasters That Have Caused Riders to Black Out**

  - Some extreme coasters have **so much force** that riders briefly **black out** during certain parts of the ride.
  - *Intimidator 305* (Kings Dominion) is known for its **extreme G-forces**, which can cause a "gray-out" effect in riders due to the intense speed and turns.

While these forces can be intense, roller coaster designers work hard to **ensure safety while maximizing thrills**.

Testing G-Forces Before a Ride Opens

Before a roller coaster is ready for riders, engineers **test G-forces** using **dummy riders and simulations**.

- **How Test Dummies Are Used**

  - Engineers place **water-filled test dummies** in the seats to **simulate human weight**.
  - These dummies help measure how forces will affect real riders.

- **Computer Simulations**
  - Every coaster is designed and tested **on a computer first**.
  - Simulations show **where G-forces will be strongest** and help designers make adjustments.
- **Why Some Coasters Are Reworked Before Opening**
  - If test results show **G-forces that are too high**, designers might need to **change the track layout** before the ride opens.
  - Some coasters, like *Son of Beast*, had to be **modified or closed down** due to extreme G-forces causing discomfort.

Testing ensures that every roller coaster delivers **maximum excitement while staying safe for riders**.

Riding the Forces of Fun

G-forces are what make roller coasters **thrilling, intense, and unpredictable**. Whether you love the feeling of being **pushed into your seat** or the **sensation of floating through the air**, G-forces create the excitement that makes roller coasters unforgettable.

- **Positive Gs push riders down, creating strong forces.**
- **Negative Gs lift riders up, creating airtime and weightlessness.**
- **Lateral Gs make sharp turns feel extra thrilling.**
- **Engineers carefully design coasters to balance intensity and fun.**

Next time you ride a roller coaster, think about the **forces at work**—because every twist, drop, and turn is designed to give you the ultimate thrill!

Chapter 8: The Mechanics of a Roller Coaster

The Hidden Technology Behind the Ride

Roller coasters may feel wild and unpredictable when you're riding them, but behind the thrills, they rely on **carefully engineered mechanics** that keep them moving smoothly and safely. Unlike cars, roller coasters **don't have engines** inside the trains—so how do they move?

Most coasters operate purely on **gravity and momentum**, but some use **advanced launch systems** to power them forward. The secret is in **how the track, wheels, and braking systems work together** to create speed, turns, and thrilling drops.

- **Why Certain Sections of a Ride Speed Up or Slow Down**
    - Coasters start with a **big drop or a powerful launch** to build momentum.
    - As the ride continues, energy is lost due to **friction and air resistance**, so engineers design the track to **use that energy efficiently**.
    - Brakes, trim brakes, and magnetic slowing systems ensure the ride doesn't go too fast in certain areas.

Every loop, twist, and drop is designed with **precision** to keep the ride thrilling but controlled.

The Track System

The track is one of the most important parts of a roller coaster—it **guides the train, controls speed, and determines how the ride feels**. There are two main types of tracks:

- **Steel Tracks**

  - Made from **smooth, tubular steel**, allowing for **loops, corkscrews, and sharp turns**.
  - Provide a **smoother ride** with less shaking compared to wooden coasters.
  - Example: *Millennium Force* (Cedar Point) has a steel track that allows for **fast, fluid motion**.

- **Wooden Tracks**

  - Built using **stacked wooden beams with a steel rail on top**.
  - Give a **rougher, bouncier ride** with more shaking and creaking sounds.
  - Can't handle extreme loops, but provide exciting **"out-of-control" airtime**.
  - Example: *The Beast* (Kings Island), a legendary wooden coaster known for its **fast turns in the woods**.

- **Hybrid Tracks (Steel and Wood Mix)**

  - Some coasters use **wooden supports with a steel track**, offering the **best of both worlds**—the excitement of wooden coasters with the smoothness of steel.
  - Example: *Steel Vengeance* (Cedar Point) is a hybrid coaster with intense **airtime and inversions**.

The **shape of the track rails** also matters—modern coasters use **precisely curved rails** to keep movement smooth and comfortable.

How the Trains Work

A roller coaster train isn't just a set of cars connected together—it's a **complex piece of machinery** designed for both **thrill and safety**.

The Three Types of Wheels That Keep Coasters Safe

1. **Running Wheels** – Sit **on top of the track**, controlling the train's movement.
2. **Side Wheels** – Hold the train **in place on turns**, preventing side-to-side motion.
3. **Underfriction Wheels (Upstop Wheels)** – Grip **below the track**, ensuring the train **stays locked in place**, even when upside down.

These **three sets of wheels work together** to keep the train securely on the track at all times, even during high-speed inversions.

Why Roller Coasters Never Fly Off the Track

- The **underfriction wheels** act as a **safety lock**, keeping the train secured to the track.
- **Gravity and physics** ensure the train has enough momentum to **stay pressed against the track** even during loops.
- Engineers test coasters extensively to **ensure no unsafe forces are at play**.

Even the wildest roller coasters are designed to be **incredibly safe**, thanks to these advanced wheel systems.

How Coasters Are Powered

Since roller coasters don't have **engines**, they rely on **external forces** to get moving. There are several ways coasters gain speed at the start of a ride:

- **Chain Lifts (Traditional Method)**

  - A **giant metal chain** pulls the train up the first hill.
  - Once the train reaches the top, gravity takes over and propels it through the rest of the ride.
  - Found on most **classic wooden and steel coasters**.
  - Example: *The Beast* (Kings Island) uses a long chain lift to build excitement before its **huge drop into the woods**.
- **Launch Mechanisms (Modern Method)**

  - Instead of a slow climb, launch coasters **blast riders forward at high speeds** in seconds.
  - Two common launch types:
    - **Hydraulic Launch** – Uses **pressurized fluid and cables** to catapult the train forward. *(Example: Kingda Ka, which reaches 128 mph in 3.5 seconds!)*
    - **Magnetic Launch (LSM or LIM)** – Uses **powerful electromagnets** to push and pull the train smoothly. *(Example: VelociCoaster at Universal Orlando.)*
- **Magnetic Propulsion (Energy-Efficient Option)**

  - Many modern coasters use **magnetism to move and slow down trains** instead of mechanical brakes.
  - Example: *Pantheon* at Busch Gardens Williamsburg uses multiple magnetic launches instead of a traditional lift hill.

These different launch systems allow coasters to create unique **thrills right from the start**, whether it's a **slow climb with suspense** or an **instant, high-speed takeoff**.

Keeping a Coaster Running

Roller coasters **undergo daily inspections** to make sure they are **operating safely** and **ready for riders**.

- **How Maintenance Crews Inspect and Repair Coasters**

    - Every morning, **technicians walk the track** looking for signs of wear or damage.
    - **Trains are tested without passengers** to ensure everything runs smoothly.
    - Engineers check **brakes, wheels, and safety restraints** before the park opens.
- **What Happens When a Coaster Temporarily Stops?**

    - If a roller coaster stops mid-ride, it's usually due to **safety sensors** detecting something unusual.
    - Ride operators **can manually restart the ride** or evacuate passengers safely if needed.
    - Many coasters **have multiple block sections** where trains automatically stop if another train is ahead, preventing collisions.
- **What If a Coaster Gets Stuck on a Lift Hill?**

    - Chain lift coasters have **safety mechanisms** that lock trains in place if they stop.
    - Ride operators can **slowly bring trains down or use emergency walkways** to evacuate riders.

Even when coasters experience small delays, **safety is always the priority**—rides are designed with **multiple backup systems** to ensure smooth operation.

Engineering the Ultimate Ride

Roller coasters might seem like **wild, unpredictable machines**, but they are actually **incredibly precise and carefully controlled**. Every track curve, train movement, and launch system is designed for **maximum excitement and safety**.

- **Track systems** keep trains moving smoothly, whether steel, wooden, or hybrid.
- **Wheel systems** ensure trains stay secure, even when upside down.
- **Different power systems** (chain lifts, launches, and magnets) give coasters their unique starts.
- **Daily inspections** keep rides running at peak performance.

The next time you ride a roller coaster, take a moment to appreciate the **engineering and mechanics at work**—because behind every thrill is a carefully crafted design that makes it all possible!

Chapter 9: Why You Don't Fall Out

How Safety Restraints Work

One of the most common fears people have about roller coasters is **falling out**—especially during high-speed drops, loops, and upside-down twists. But thanks to **carefully designed safety restraints**, riders stay securely in place no matter how intense the ride gets.

There are several types of safety restraints used on roller coasters:

- **Lap Bars**

    - A padded bar that locks over a rider's lap, holding them in place.
    - Common on wooden coasters and hyper coasters (rides over 200 feet tall).
    - Example: *Millennium Force* at Cedar Point uses only a lap bar, allowing for **maximum airtime** while keeping riders safe.
- **Over-the-Shoulder Restraints (OTSRs)**

    - A harness that locks over the shoulders, often with a chest or waist buckle.
    - Used on **looping and inverted coasters** to keep riders from moving during inversions.
    - Example: *The Incredible Hulk Coaster* at Universal Orlando.
- **Seat Belts**

    - Often used **in addition to lap bars** as a secondary safety feature.
    - Some parks, like **Disney**, require seat belts on nearly all rides as an extra precaution.

How do restraints lock in place?

- Most modern restraints use a **ratcheting system** or **hydraulics** to ensure they **stay locked** throughout the ride.
- The ride's computer system **checks and double-checks** that all restraints are secured before the train can launch.

Even if a restraint **feels loose**, it is designed to **hold riders safely in their seats**, no matter how extreme the ride.

The Physics of Staying in Your Seat

Even without restraints, physics alone would keep most riders from falling out of a coaster. This is due to two important forces:

- **Momentum (Keeps You Moving Forward)**

  - When a roller coaster train speeds through the track, your body **naturally follows that motion**.
  - Even when going upside down, your body is still being **pushed forward along the track**, not downward.
- **Centripetal Force (Pushes You Into Your Seat)**

  - When you go through a loop, the train is moving so fast that it creates a force **pushing you into your seat, not pulling you out**.
  - This is why riders never feel like they're going to "fall" when they're upside down—**the force is pressing them downward into the train, not up toward the sky**.

This is also why **roller coaster loops are teardrop-shaped, not circular**—a circular loop would create too much force at the bottom and **not enough at the top**, making it unsafe.

As long as the **coaster is moving fast enough through the inversion**, physics alone would **hold you in place**, even if there were no restraints!

Real vs. Imaginary Danger

Even though roller coasters are incredibly safe, our brains **sometimes trick us** into thinking we're in danger. Many coasters are designed to make **riders feel like they're about to fall**, even when they're completely secure.

- **Why You Feel Like You Might Fall Out (But Won't)**

  - Airtime hills create a sense of **floating or lifting out of your seat**, which can feel risky—but lap bars ensure riders are never actually in danger.
  - Sideways banked turns feel **unnatural**, making riders believe they might "tip out," but the train's wheels and track shape keep everything in place.
  - Inverted coasters, where riders hang **below the track**, create a sense of exposure, but **shoulder restraints lock tightly in place**.
- **"Tricks" Coasters Use to Feel Scarier Than They Are**

  - **Sharp near-misses:** Coasters are designed to make riders think they might **hit an object**, but everything is perfectly calculated to give **just enough clearance**.

- Drop tracks: Some rides, like *Verbolten* at Busch Gardens, **suddenly drop riders vertically**, creating the illusion of **free-fall**.
- Fake-out turns: Some coasters, like *Expedition Everest*, trick riders by making them think they're going one way, only to suddenly **switch directions**.

Even though roller coasters feel **wild and unpredictable**, every element is **carefully controlled for safety**.

Testing Safety Before Riders Get On

Before a roller coaster can open each day, it **undergoes strict safety checks** to make sure everything is running smoothly.

- **Daily Inspections**

    - Every morning, maintenance crews **walk the track**, checking for **any signs of wear** or loose bolts.
    - Restraints, brakes, and sensors are **tested multiple times** before the first riders get on.
    - **Test trains run through the entire ride empty** to ensure **everything operates correctly**.
- **Weight Distribution Checks**

    - Roller coasters perform best when the train has a **balanced weight distribution**.
    - Sometimes, ride operators may ask certain riders to **switch seats** to keep the weight even.
- **Emergency Stops and Safety Sensors**

    - If a roller coaster detects **anything unusual**, it will **automatically stop** before continuing the ride.

- Operators have **override controls** but **cannot start a ride unless all safety checks pass**.

These safety measures **ensure that every rider is secure before the ride even begins**.

The History of Roller Coaster Safety

Over the years, roller coaster safety has **greatly improved**. Early coasters had **fewer restraints and looser regulations**, but thanks to modern technology, today's rides are safer than ever.

- **Early Coaster Safety (1900s-1950s)**

    - The first roller coasters had **no seat belts or restraints**—riders simply held onto a metal bar!
    - Coasters were **slower and less extreme**, so restraints weren't as necessary.
    - Example: *Leap-The-Dips* (1902) is the **oldest operating coaster** and still has no restraints today.
- **The Introduction of Lap Bars and Over-the-Shoulder Restraints (1960s-1980s)**

    - As coasters got taller and faster, **lap bars and seat belts** became standard.
    - The first major **over-the-shoulder harness** was introduced in the 1970s for looping coasters.
- **Modern Safety Features (1990s-Present)**

    - **Hydraulic and magnetic restraints** ensure smooth, secure locking mechanisms.
    - **Computer monitoring systems** check every seat's restraint before dispatch.

- New ride materials (like hybrid steel-wood coasters) allow for safer, smoother experiences.

Today, roller coasters **undergo years of testing** before they ever open to the public, ensuring **every element is safe and secure.**

A Ride Designed for Safety

While roller coasters **feel risky**, they are actually some of the **safest rides in the world.** Thanks to **physics, safety restraints, and advanced testing**, falling out of a roller coaster is nearly impossible.

- **Lap bars, harnesses, and seat belts keep riders locked in place.**
- **Momentum and centripetal force push riders into their seats, even upside down.**
- **Illusions make rides feel scarier than they are—but they're carefully engineered for safety.**
- **Daily safety checks ensure that every ride is operating at peak performance.**

The next time you're on a roller coaster and feel like you might fall out, remember—**everything is designed to keep you safely in your seat, no matter how wild the ride gets!**

Chapter 10: Building a Roller Coaster

The Design Process

Every roller coaster starts as an **idea on paper**, but bringing that idea to life is a complex process that takes **years of planning, engineering, and testing**. Designing a roller coaster isn't just about making a ride thrilling—it also has to be **safe, comfortable, and exciting** for riders of all ages.

1. **Concept and Layout**

   - Engineers and designers brainstorm ride ideas based on **thrill level, space, and budget**.
   - The team decides on key features like **height, inversions, speed, and track length**.
   - A **layout is drawn**, showing where the ride will twist, turn, drop, and loop.

2. **Using Computer Simulations**

   - Once a general layout is decided, engineers create **3D computer models** of the ride.
   - These simulations help test **G-forces, speed, and rider comfort** before anything is built.
   - Special software predicts how the train will move and ensures the forces won't be too strong or unsafe for riders.

3. **Prototyping and Approval**

   - Engineers build **small-scale models** of key elements to test how they work.
   - Parks work with **roller coaster manufacturers** to finalize the design.
   - Once everything is approved, **construction begins**—but that's only the start!

Building a roller coaster is a long process that requires careful **planning, physics, and creativity** to ensure every turn and drop feels just right.

Choosing the Perfect Location

Before construction can begin, amusement parks must decide **where to build the ride**. Location matters because it affects how **big, loud, and exciting** the ride can be.

- **Space and Terrain**

    - Some coasters need **huge open spaces** (like *Fury 325* at Carowinds), while others are built in **small areas** with tight turns (like *The Smiler* in the UK).
    - Some coasters use the **natural landscape** to enhance the ride, like *The Beast* at Kings Island, which winds through a forest.
- **Theming and Park Atmosphere**

    - Coasters need to **fit the theme of the park**.
    - A thrill park like **Six Flags** might build a **record-breaking coaster**, while Disney focuses on **story-driven, immersive rides** like *Expedition Everest*.
- **Challenges of Building in Tight Spaces**

    - Some parks have limited land, so designers create **compact coasters** that use vertical space instead of sprawling tracks.
    - Example: *The Incredible Hulk Coaster* at Universal Orlando was built **above walkways** to maximize space.

Finding the right spot is crucial—it ensures the coaster fits **within the park's landscape, theme, and ride lineup**.

The Construction Process

Once the design is finalized and the location is chosen, construction crews get to work. Building a roller coaster is a **massive project** that involves precise engineering.

1. **Laying the Foundation**

   - The first step is creating a strong **foundation**.
   - Concrete footers are poured into the ground to hold the coaster's **supports in place**.

2. **Assembling the Track and Supports**

   - Track pieces arrive **in sections** and are carefully **lifted into place** by cranes.
   - Supports are bolted to footers, ensuring they align perfectly with the track.
   - For tall coasters like *Kingda Ka*, massive **steel towers** must be constructed piece by piece.

3. **Installing the Ride System**

   - Once the track is finished, **wheels, brakes, and sensors** are installed.
   - Electrical and **computer control systems** are added to **monitor safety and ride operations**.

Everything must be **precisely measured and secured**—even a tiny misalignment can cause major problems when the ride is tested.

How Coasters Are Tested Before Opening

Before letting riders on, a roller coaster must pass **weeks of testing** to ensure it is safe, smooth, and thrilling.

1. **First Test Runs Without Riders**

   - Engineers send empty trains through the track to check for **smoothness, speed, and braking accuracy**.
   - Water-filled test dummies are used to **simulate real riders' weight**.

2. **Gradually Increasing Ride Speeds**

   - Some coasters **start running slower** to ensure all parts are working correctly.
   - Adjustments are made to **brakes, wheels, and launch speeds** before finalizing the ride experience.

3. **Government and Safety Inspections**

   - Every new coaster must **pass strict safety inspections** before opening to the public.
   - Parks conduct **test rides with employees and engineers** before allowing guests on.

This **extensive testing process** ensures that the ride is not just thrilling but also **perfectly safe and reliable**.

What It's Like to Be a Roller Coaster Engineer

Have you ever wondered what it takes to **design and build** roller coasters? Roller coaster engineers work in **a mix of physics, engineering, and creativity** to develop the rides we love.

Skills Needed to Design Roller Coasters

- **Strong math and physics knowledge** (to calculate forces and energy).
- **Mechanical engineering skills** (to understand structures, wheels, and brakes).
- **Creativity** (to design unique and exciting ride layouts).

How Engineers Come Up With New Ride Ideas

- Some engineers study **existing coasters** to find ways to improve ride experiences.
- Others invent **brand-new ride concepts**, like *flying coasters* (where riders lay face-down) or *spinning coasters* (where cars rotate).
- Engineers also test **new materials** to make coasters **smoother, taller, and faster** than ever before.

Famous roller coaster manufacturers like **Bolliger & Mabillard (B&M), Intamin, and Rocky Mountain Construction (RMC)** are always pushing the limits of **thrill ride technology**.

From Blueprints to Thrill Rides

Building a roller coaster is a **long, complex process**, but the result is a **thrilling, unforgettable experience** for riders.

- It all starts with **an idea** that is carefully designed using **computer simulations**.
- Engineers work with **amusement parks** to find the perfect location and layout.
- Construction crews **assemble the track, install the system, and test the ride extensively** before it opens.
- Roller coaster engineers combine **science, engineering, and creativity** to create the next big thrill ride.

The next time you're strapped into a roller coaster, remember—it took **years of work, planning, and testing** to bring that ride to life!

Chapter 11: The Best Amusement Parks for Coasters

Introduction to Amusement Parks

Roller coasters can be found in **theme parks and amusement parks** all over the world, but not all parks are created equal when it comes to thrill rides. Some parks are famous for their **record-breaking coasters**, while others focus on immersive storytelling or unique ride experiences.

What makes an amusement park great for roller coasters?

- **Variety** – Parks with a mix of wooden, steel, looping, and launch coasters offer something for every thrill seeker.
- **Record-breaking rides** – Some parks are home to the world's **tallest, fastest, and most intense** coasters.
- **Innovative designs** – The best parks work with top coaster manufacturers to create **one-of-a-kind ride experiences**.

But what's the difference between **theme parks** and **traditional amusement parks**?

- **Theme Parks** (Disney, Universal, Busch Gardens) focus on **immersive storytelling**, blending roller coasters with **detailed worlds, special effects, and interactive elements**.
- **Traditional Amusement Parks** (Cedar Point, Six Flags) focus on **thrill rides**, with a strong emphasis on **record-breaking coasters and high-adrenaline attractions**.

Now, let's explore some of the **best parks for roller coaster fans** around the world!

Top Roller Coaster Parks in the U.S.

The United States is home to some of the **biggest and best roller coaster parks** on the planet. These parks are known for their **thrill-packed lineups** and **legendary coasters**.

- **Cedar Point (Ohio) – "The Roller Coaster Capital of the World"**

  - Home to **17 world-class roller coasters**, including record-breaking rides.
  - Notable coasters: *Millennium Force* (the first giga coaster), *Steel Vengeance* (a hybrid airtime machine), and *Top Thrill 2* (a multi-launch strata coaster).
  - Known for **lakefront views, massive coasters, and a perfect mix of old and new rides.**

- **Six Flags Magic Mountain (California) – Most Roller Coasters in One Park**

  - Holds the record for **most roller coasters in a single park (20+ rides!)**.
  - Notable coasters: *X2* (4D spinning coaster), *Twisted Colossus* (dueling hybrid coaster), and *Tatsu* (a flying coaster).
  - A paradise for **thrill seekers who love extreme and high-speed rides.**

- **Busch Gardens Williamsburg (Virginia) – The Most Beautiful Coaster Park**

  - Blends **themed lands based on European countries** with top-tier coasters.
  - Notable coasters: *Pantheon* (multi-launch coaster), *Apollo's Chariot* (hyper coaster), and *Griffon* (a 205-foot drop coaster).
  - Perfect for **coaster fans who also love detailed park theming.**

- **Hersheypark (Pennsylvania) – Chocolate and Coasters**

    - A **family-friendly coaster park** with a strong mix of thrills.
    - Notable coasters: *Skyrush* (extreme airtime coaster), *Candymonium* (smooth hyper coaster), and *Storm Runner* (powerful launch coaster).
    - Bonus: You can visit the **Hershey's Chocolate World** for free samples!

Other top U.S. coaster parks:

- **Kings Island (Ohio)** – Home to *The Beast*, the longest wooden coaster in the world.
- **Carowinds (North Carolina/South Carolina)** – Features *Fury 325*, one of the **tallest and fastest coasters** in the world.
- **Dollywood (Tennessee)** – A **scenic mountain park** with exciting coasters like *Lightning Rod*, the world's first launched wooden coaster.

These parks are **must-visit locations for coaster enthusiasts** who love **fast, intense, and high-energy rides**.

Best International Parks for Roller Coasters

Roller coasters aren't just a U.S. phenomenon—some of the **most extreme and innovative coasters** can be found in amusement parks across the world.

- **Fuji-Q Highland (Japan) – The Most Intense Coasters in One Park**

- Home to **some of the scariest rides on the planet**, with record-breaking speeds and heights.
- Notable coasters:
    - *Dodonpa* (insane **launch coaster** that accelerates to 112 mph in 1.6 seconds!).
    - *Eejanaika* (a **4D coaster** with spinning seats).
    - *Takabisha* (the world's **steepest roller coaster**, with a 121-degree drop).

- **Europa Park (Germany) – The Best Themed Coaster Park in Europe**

    - Features **different lands based on European countries**, blending **theming and thrill rides**.
    - Notable coasters:
        - *Silver Star* (hyper coaster with high speeds and airtime).
        - *Blue Fire* (launched coaster with inversions and a smooth ride).

- **Canada's Wonderland (Canada) – The Biggest Coaster Park in Canada**

    - Home to some of the **biggest and fastest coasters in North America**.
    - Notable coasters: *Leviathan* (giga coaster) and *Yukon Striker* (the longest, fastest dive coaster in the world).

Other great international coaster parks:

- **Tivoli Gardens (Denmark) –** One of the **oldest amusement parks**, featuring classic coasters.
- **Energylandia (Poland) –** An **up-and-coming coaster park** with **more than 20 roller coasters**.
- **Nagashima Spa Land (Japan) –** Home to *Steel Dragon 2000*, the **longest roller coaster in the world**.

For coaster fans willing to travel, these parks **offer one-of-a-kind rides and experiences** not found anywhere else.

Disney vs. Universal: The Themed Coaster Battle

While **Disney** and **Universal** may not focus on **record-breaking thrills**, they have some of the most **well-designed and immersive roller coasters in the world.**

- **Best Disney Coasters:**

    - *Space Mountain* – A classic indoor coaster in complete darkness.
    - *Tron Lightcycle Run* – A high-speed, neon-lit motorbike coaster.
    - *Expedition Everest* – A detailed mountain coaster with **a surprise track switch.**
- **Best Universal Coasters:**

    - *VelociCoaster* – One of the **most intense and well-themed launch coasters ever built.**
    - *The Incredible Hulk Coaster* – A powerful **launch coaster** with **seven inversions.**
    - *Hagrid's Magical Creatures Motorbike Adventure* – A **story-driven coaster** with surprises, including a **drop track section.**

While Disney rides focus more on **family-friendly thrills,** Universal rides tend to be **faster, taller, and more extreme. Both parks offer unforgettable coaster experiences!**

Underrated Parks with Great Coasters

Some of the best roller coasters **aren't in massive, well-known parks**—here are some **hidden gems** worth checking out.

- **Holiday World (Indiana)** – Home to *The Voyage*, one of the best wooden coasters in the world.
- **Silver Dollar City (Missouri)** – Features *Time Traveler*, a **launched spinning coaster**.
- **Knoebels (Pennsylvania)** – Home to *Phoenix*, a classic wooden coaster with some of the **best airtime anywhere**.

These parks might not be as famous, but they **deliver some of the most exciting coaster experiences in the world**.

Where Will You Ride Next?

Whether you love **high-speed thrill rides, themed coaster experiences**, or **record-breaking drops**, there's an amusement park for every roller coaster fan.

- **Cedar Point and Six Flags Magic Mountain** are perfect for **extreme thrill seekers**.
- **Fuji-Q Highland and Europa Park** offer **incredible international rides**.
- **Disney and Universal focus on storytelling with world-class coaster technology**.

No matter where you go, these parks prove one thing: **there's always a bigger, faster, or more exciting roller coaster waiting for you!**

Chapter 12: Planning the Perfect Park Visit

Visiting an amusement park filled with roller coasters is one of the most exciting experiences for any thrill-seeker. But to make the most of your trip, **a little planning goes a long way.** A poorly planned visit can lead to long waits, missed rides, and exhaustion, while a well-planned trip ensures maximum fun and non-stop thrills.

How to Plan Your Roller Coaster Adventure

Before heading to an amusement park, it's important to **choose the right park** and prepare in advance.

- **Picking the Right Park**

  - If you love **extreme thrills**, visit **Cedar Point, Six Flags Magic Mountain, or Fuji-Q Highland** for record-breaking coasters.
  - If you prefer **immersive experiences**, check out **Disney, Universal, or Europa Park** for themed roller coasters with storytelling elements.
  - If you enjoy **classic coasters**, visit **Hersheypark, Kings Island, or Knoebels** for legendary wooden and steel rides.
- **Check Ride Height Requirements**

  - Every roller coaster has a **minimum height requirement**, usually between **48" and 54"**.
  - Some parks have an **official website or app** where you can check **which rides you're eligible to ride.**
- **Look at Park Maps and Ride Locations in Advance**

- Familiarizing yourself with the park layout can save time once you arrive.
- Some coasters are at the **back of the park**, so knowing where they are can help **plan your route efficiently.**

Doing some basic research before your trip can make **your visit smoother and stress-free**, ensuring you ride as many coasters as possible.

Beating the Crowds

Long lines can **ruin an amusement park trip**, but there are ways to **reduce wait times** and **maximize your ride count.**

- **Arrive Early (Before the Park Opens!)**

  - Many parks allow **early entry**, especially for season pass holders.
  - Getting there before the gates open **lets you ride the most popular coasters first with little to no wait.**
- **Use Fast Passes and Single Rider Lines**

  - Some parks offer **fast passes** (like Disney's Lightning Lane or Six Flags' Flash Pass) to skip the longest lines.
  - Many coasters have **single rider lines**, which allow you to fill empty seats faster than waiting in the normal queue.
- **Use Mobile Apps to Check Wait Times**

  - Many parks have official apps that provide **live ride wait times**, helping you **plan which coasters to ride next.**

- Example: *Universal's app lets you see which rides have the shortest wait and adjust your route accordingly.*

By **strategically planning your rides**, you can avoid **standing in line all day** and instead **spend your time riding as many coasters as possible.**

Making the Most of Your Day

With so many coasters to ride, it's important to **have a strategy** so you don't **wear yourself out too early.**

- **Ride the Biggest Coasters First**

    - Head straight to the park's **most popular roller coaster** at opening.
    - The best strategy is:
        - **Ride the biggest coasters first** (while the lines are shortest).
        - **Move on to medium-sized rides** as crowds start to arrive.
        - **Repeat your favorite rides later in the day** when crowds thin out.
- **Mix in Other Attractions to Avoid Exhaustion**

    - If you ride **back-to-back intense coasters**, you might **get tired or dizzy quickly.**
    - Break up your day by:
        - **Riding slower attractions** (log flumes, dark rides, Ferris wheels) between major coasters.
        - **Taking food breaks** to rest and recharge.

- **Exploring the park's unique attractions**, like live shows or themed areas.

Following this **balance of thrill rides and breaks** will help you **last the entire day** without feeling exhausted.

What to Bring to the Park

Packing the right essentials can make a **huge difference** in your amusement park experience.

Must-Have Items for a Fun and Comfortable Day

■ **Comfortable Walking Shoes** – You'll be on your feet all day. Avoid flip-flops or sandals.

■ **Sunscreen and Sunglasses** – Parks are mostly outdoors, and sunburn can ruin your trip.

■ **Refillable Water Bottle** – Staying hydrated is key! Many parks allow **free water refills**.

■ **Lightweight Backpack or Fanny Pack** – To carry essentials without weighing you down.

■ **Phone and Portable Charger** – Many parks have mobile apps, so you'll need battery life to check wait times.

■ **Cash/Card for Food and Souvenirs** – Some parks have cashless payment, so check before visiting.

What to Avoid Bringing

🚫 **Loose Items (Hats, Glasses, Phones in Hand)** – These can **fly off on fast rides**.

🚫 **Large Bags or Heavy Backpacks** – Many coasters **require lockers** for large bags, so keep it light.

🚫 **Expensive Electronics** – Unless necessary, leave tablets, cameras, and laptops at home.

Most parks **have lockers available**, but keeping your items **light and secure** makes for a **hassle-free** experience.

Staying Safe and Having Fun

Roller coasters are exciting, but to **enjoy the whole day without feeling sick or exhausted**, here are some important tips:

- **Stay Hydrated and Take Breaks**

    - Dehydration can cause **headaches and dizziness**, so **drink water regularly**.
    - Take a break in the **shade or an air-conditioned area** if you start feeling overheated.
- **Avoid Motion Sickness**

    - If you get motion sick easily, try these tricks:
        - Ride **in the front row** (the back can be rougher).
        - **Eat light meals**—avoid heavy food before big coasters.
        - Take **motion sickness medicine** before arriving if needed.
- **How to Handle Long Lines Without Getting Bored**

    - **Play games** (many parks have interactive app games for guests).
    - **Chat with friends or family** about the next ride.
    - **Watch other riders** to get excited for your turn.

By **staying hydrated, pacing yourself, and handling wait times wisely**, you'll have **an amazing day from start to finish**.

A Perfect Day of Thrills

Planning ahead **makes all the difference** when visiting an amusement park. Instead of wandering aimlessly or **spending hours in long lines**, a good strategy ensures **non-stop fun and more time on the rides you love.**

- Pick the **right park** based on the type of roller coasters you love.
- Arrive **early** and use **fast passes or single rider lines** to beat the crowds.
- Ride the **biggest coasters first**, then balance your day with food, shows, and smaller attractions.
- Bring **essentials like comfortable shoes, sunscreen, and a refillable water bottle.**
- Stay **hydrated, take breaks when needed, and enjoy every ride to the fullest.**

With these tips, you'll be ready to experience **the ultimate roller coaster adventure**—and maybe even set a personal record for **most coasters ridden in a day!**

Chapter 13: Roller Coaster Safety

Roller coasters are designed to feel **fast, thrilling, and even a little dangerous**, but the truth is that they are one of the **safest forms of entertainment** in the world. Every ride operates under strict safety guidelines, daily inspections, and advanced technology to ensure every rider has an exciting but secure experience.

How Safe Are Roller Coasters?

Many people assume roller coasters are risky, but statistics show that **riding a roller coaster is far safer than many everyday activities**.

- The **chances of being seriously injured on a roller coaster** are about **1 in 15.5 million.**
- More people get **injured playing sports, riding bicycles, or driving a car** than on amusement park rides.
- Roller coasters are **designed, tested, and inspected** to meet **strict safety standards** set by government agencies and independent engineers.

Even though they feel intense, modern roller coasters are built to **deliver thrills while keeping riders completely safe.**

How Rides Are Inspected Daily

Before a park opens each day, every roller coaster goes through **a thorough inspection process** to ensure it is in perfect working condition.

- **Morning Safety Checks**

  - Engineers **walk the entire track**, looking for any signs of wear or damage.
  - The **train's wheels, restraints, and braking systems** are inspected to make sure they are functioning correctly.
  - Sensors, launch systems, and electrical components are tested for **proper response times**.
- **Test Runs Without Passengers**

  - Before riders are allowed on, **empty test trains** run multiple times to confirm the ride is operating smoothly.
  - Water-filled test dummies are sometimes used to simulate **real passenger weight**.
- **What Happens If a Ride Fails an Inspection?**

  - If an issue is found, the ride remains **closed for maintenance** until the problem is fixed.
  - Parks have **backup parts on hand** to quickly replace faulty components.
  - A ride **will not open until all safety standards are met**, even if it means delaying its operation for the day.

These safety checks ensure that **every rider gets a secure and thrilling experience without any risks**.

Safety Rules Every Rider Should Follow

Even though roller coasters are extremely safe, **riders must follow the rules** to ensure their own safety. Many ride accidents happen **because people ignore safety guidelines**.

- **Keep Hands, Arms, and Legs Inside the Ride**

    - Sticking hands or feet out can result in **injuries** if they hit nearby objects or track supports.
- **Follow Height and Weight Restrictions**

    - These rules exist to **keep riders safe** based on how the restraint systems work.
    - If a rider is **too short, too tall, or outside the weight limits**, they may not be properly secured in their seat.
- **Always Wear Restraints Correctly**

    - Riders should **never try to loosen, unlock, or adjust their restraints** during the ride.
    - If a restraint feels loose, notify a ride operator before the ride starts.
- **Listen to Ride Operators**

    - Ride operators give **important safety instructions** before dispatching the train.
    - Disregarding instructions can **delay the ride or result in removal from the park**.

Following these rules helps ensure that **every ride remains safe and enjoyable for all guests**.

Emergency Stops and Evacuations

Sometimes, roller coasters **temporarily stop** due to weather conditions, ride sensors, or technical issues. While it may feel scary, **emergency stops and evacuations are completely safe** and handled by trained park employees.

- **What Happens If a Roller Coaster Gets Stuck?**

- Many modern coasters have **safety brake sections** that can **pause the ride if needed**.
- If a coaster stops, **ride operators and maintenance teams assess the situation** before restarting the ride.
- In most cases, the ride resumes normally after a brief pause.

- **How Park Employees Handle Ride Evacuations**

  - If a ride cannot be restarted, **park staff will evacuate passengers calmly and safely**.
  - Emergency walkways, stairs, and platforms are built into coasters for easy exit if needed.
  - Employees are trained to **guide riders step-by-step**, ensuring no one is ever in danger.

Stopping mid-ride may feel nerve-wracking, but coasters have **multiple backup safety features** in place to keep riders **secure in every situation**.

Myths and Misconceptions About Coaster Safety

Many people have **irrational fears** about roller coasters, but most of these fears come from **misconceptions rather than reality**.

- **Myth: You Can Fall Out of a Roller Coaster**

  - Reality: **Centripetal force and secure restraints** keep riders safely in their seats, even when upside down.
  - Coaster trains are designed with **multi-layered safety systems**, including lap bars, over-the-shoulder restraints, and upstop wheels that prevent them from leaving the track.

- **Myth: People Frequently Black Out on Coasters**

  - Reality: While some coasters create **high G-forces**, they are designed **not to exceed safe limits**.
  - Feeling lightheaded (or experiencing a "gray-out") can happen temporarily on intense rides but is **not dangerous**.
- **Myth: Getting Stuck Upside Down is a Serious Risk**

  - Reality: Modern roller coasters **rarely, if ever, get stuck upside down**.
  - Most **stoppages happen on lift hills, brake runs, or straight track sections**, not in loops.
- **Myth: Roller Coasters Are Unsafe for Your Health**

  - Reality: Roller coasters are designed for **a wide range of people**, and amusement parks work with **medical experts** to set safety standards.
  - People with **heart conditions, high blood pressure, or pregnancy** are advised not to ride extreme coasters, but for most healthy individuals, coasters **pose no health risks**.

Modern roller coasters are **safer than ever before**, thanks to **cutting-edge technology and strict safety regulations**.

A Thrilling Ride Without the Risk

Roller coasters may seem dangerous, but they are actually **one of the safest forms of entertainment in the world**. Thanks to **daily inspections, advanced safety features, and well-trained ride operators**, riders can experience thrilling speeds, loops, and drops with complete confidence.

- Parks conduct **thorough safety checks** every morning before opening.
- **Restraints and ride designs keep passengers secure**, even on the most extreme coasters.
- **Emergency stops and evacuations** are handled professionally and safely.
- Many common fears about roller coasters are based on **myths rather than facts**.

The next time you buckle into a roller coaster, remember—you are riding on a **carefully engineered thrill machine that is designed to be both exciting and completely safe**.

Chapter 14: Becoming a Roller Coaster Enthusiast

Some people visit amusement parks just for a fun day out, while others make roller coasters their **passion**. Roller coaster enthusiasts are more than just thrill-seekers—they travel to different parks, ride as many coasters as possible, and learn about the history and engineering behind these rides. If you love coasters and want to take your interest to the next level, this chapter will guide you on how to **become a true roller coaster enthusiast**.

What Is a Roller Coaster Enthusiast?

A roller coaster enthusiast is someone who:

- Rides **as many different roller coasters as possible.**
- Learns about the **history, engineering, and mechanics of coasters.**
- Keeps track of their **ride count, favorite parks, and top coasters.**
- Joins coaster clubs and participates in **special coaster events.**

While casual amusement park visitors may **ride a coaster and move on**, enthusiasts often:

- **Plan trips around specific roller coasters.**
- **Seek out record-breaking rides** to experience something new.
- **Compare coaster types** and discuss their favorites with fellow fans.

Many enthusiasts **travel the world** to ride unique coasters, visiting parks in different countries and experiencing rare ride designs. Whether you want to visit **every Six Flags park,**

explore classic wooden coasters, or ride every record-breaker, there's a whole community of coaster fans just like you!

Joining Coaster Clubs and Communities

One of the best ways to **connect with other roller coaster fans** is by joining coaster enthusiast groups. These clubs offer members **special perks, meetups, and behind-the-scenes access to coasters.**

Popular Roller Coaster Enthusiast Clubs

- **ACE (American Coaster Enthusiasts)** – The largest and most well-known coaster club. Members get access to **exclusive ride events, early ride times, and coaster history tours**.
- **CoasterBuzz Club** – A club for thrill seekers who want **insider coaster news and trip planning tips**.
- **European Coaster Club (ECC)** – A group for **coaster fans in Europe**, offering **group trips and special ride sessions**.

Benefits of Joining a Coaster Club

- **Exclusive Ride Events** – Many parks offer coaster clubs **early access to new rides** before the general public.
- **Behind-the-Scenes Tours** – Enthusiasts get the chance to **see how rides work** from a technical perspective.
- **Meeting Other Coaster Fans** – Clubs provide a way to **connect with like-minded thrill seekers** who love discussing coasters.

Joining a coaster club is a great way to **take your passion to the next level** and experience theme parks in a completely new way.

Keeping Track of the Coasters You've Ridden

Many enthusiasts enjoy tracking the **number and types of coasters they've ridden**. Keeping a coaster log can help you:

- **Remember your favorites** and compare ride experiences.
- **Set coaster goals**, such as reaching a milestone like **100 different coasters**.
- **Rate and review rides** to see how your opinions change over time.

Ways to Track Your Coaster Rides

1. **Coaster Counting Apps**

   - Websites like **Coaster-Count.com** allow enthusiasts to **log every roller coaster they've ridden**.
   - Apps like **LogRide** help users track ride stats and park visits.

2. **Coaster Bucket Lists**

   - Some enthusiasts create a list of **"must-ride coasters"** and check them off as they go.
   - Popular bucket list coasters include record-holders like *Steel Vengeance*, *Kingda Ka*, and *Formula Rossa*.

3. **Rating Systems**

   - Some coaster fans **rank rides on a personal scale** (e.g., rating them from 1 to 10).

- Others **compare different ride elements**, like airtime, inversions, and smoothness.

Tracking your coasters helps **capture your experiences** and motivates you to **ride even more coasters** in the future!

Learning More About Ride Design

Roller coaster enthusiasts often want to **understand how rides are built and why they feel the way they do**. Learning about ride mechanics can make your coaster trips even more exciting.

Best Resources for Learning About Coasters

- **Books:**

  - *The Roller Coaster Lover's Companion* by Steven Urbanowicz – A deep dive into **coaster history and technology**.
  - *Theme Park Design* by Steve Alcorn – A guide to **how theme parks and rides are created**.
- **Documentaries and YouTube Channels:**

  - *The History of Roller Coasters* (PBS) – A documentary exploring the evolution of coasters.
  - **Coaster Studios (YouTube)** – Features **ride reviews, history, and theme park news**.
  - **Defunctland (YouTube)** – Covers **forgotten and closed theme park attractions**.
- **Coaster Manufacturer Websites:**

  - **Intamin, B&M, RMC, and Vekoma** provide **detailed ride specs and innovation news**.

- These companies are responsible for some of the **biggest and most advanced coasters in the world.**

Learning about **coaster design and history** helps enthusiasts appreciate **what makes each ride unique and groundbreaking.**

How to Start Riding Bigger and Scarier Coasters

If you want to become a **true coaster enthusiast**, you may need to **step outside your comfort zone** and try bigger, faster, and more extreme rides.

Tips for Overcoming Fear of Bigger Coasters

1. **Start with Medium-Intensity Coasters**

   - If looping rides seem intimidating, try **smaller steel coasters with mild inversions** first.
   - If high drops make you nervous, try coasters with **gradual airtime hills** before attempting a 300-foot drop.

2. **Ride with Friends Who Love Coasters**

   - Having **enthusiastic friends** can make the experience more fun and less intimidating.

3. **Watch POV Videos to Prepare**

   - Many parks release **front-row ride videos** online, so you can see what to expect before riding.

Why Enthusiasts Prefer Certain Coaster Types

- Some coaster fans love **wooden coasters** because they feel **classic, rough, and unpredictable.**
- Others prefer **hyper and giga coasters** for their **smooth speed and intense airtime.**
- Some riders seek out **looping coasters** because they enjoy **high G-forces and fast inversions.**

No matter what type of coaster you prefer, working your way up to **bigger and scarier rides** is a huge part of becoming a **true roller coaster enthusiast.**

Becoming a True Coaster Fan

Roller coaster enthusiasts take their love for coasters to the next level by **tracking their rides, studying coaster design, and joining coaster communities.**

- **Enthusiasts ride coasters worldwide, compare experiences, and keep detailed ride logs.**
- **Joining coaster clubs offers exclusive ride events, behind-the-scenes access, and meetups with other fans.**
- **Learning about ride mechanics deepens appreciation for roller coasters and how they work.**
- **Overcoming fears and trying bigger rides is part of the fun of being an enthusiast.**

If you love roller coasters and want to take your passion further, consider **tracking your rides, learning about coaster history, and joining a community of fellow thrill-seekers.** The next big ride is always waiting!

Chapter 15: Breaking World Records

Roller coasters are constantly pushing the limits of what's possible—going **higher, faster, longer, and more extreme** with each new ride. Around the world, amusement parks compete to build record-breaking attractions that offer riders the **biggest thrills imaginable**. From coasters that reach the **stratosphere** to those that twist riders upside down **more times than ever before**, let's explore the wildest, fastest, and most unique roller coasters that have shattered world records.

The Tallest Roller Coasters Ever Built

The race to build the world's tallest roller coaster has been **ongoing for decades**. Coasters have grown from simple wooden hills to **sky-piercing steel towers** that stand as some of the tallest structures in theme parks.

- **Kingda Ka (Six Flags Great Adventure, New Jersey, USA)**

    - **Height:** 456 feet (139 meters)
    - **Opened:** 2005
    - The **tallest roller coaster in the world** launches riders from 0 to **128 mph in just 3.5 seconds** before shooting **straight up** a 456-foot tower, cresting the top, and plummeting back down in a terrifying freefall.
- **Top Thrill 2 (Cedar Point, Ohio, USA)**

    - **Height:** 420 feet (128 meters)
    - **Opened:** 2024 (formerly Top Thrill Dragster, revamped with a new multi-launch system).
    - One of the most **iconic coasters ever built**, now featuring **two launches and a vertical**

rollback that lets riders experience insane airtime before reaching the top.

Other notable towering coasters include:

- *Red Force* (Spain) – A **367-foot launched coaster** at Ferrari Land.
- *Superman: Escape from Krypton* (California) – A **415-foot drop tower-style coaster** at Six Flags Magic Mountain.

As technology advances, coaster designers continue to **push the height record**, with rumors of future rides exceeding **500 feet**.

The Fastest Coasters on Earth

Speed is one of the most exciting factors of a roller coaster, and some rides push the limits of how fast a coaster train can travel.

- **Formula Rossa (Ferrari World, Abu Dhabi, UAE)**

  - **Speed:** 149 mph (240 km/h) – **fastest coaster in the world**.
  - **Launch System:** Hydraulic launch, similar to jet fighter technology.
  - Riders wear **goggles** to protect their eyes from **high-speed winds** as they experience G-forces similar to those felt in a Formula 1 race car.
- **Kingda Ka (Six Flags Great Adventure, New Jersey, USA)**

  - **Speed:** 128 mph (206 km/h) in just 3.5 seconds.

- The **fastest coaster in North America**, with an intense launch that feels like being shot out of a cannon.
- **Dodonpa (Fuji-Q Highland, Japan)**

  - **Speed:** 112 mph (180 km/h) in just **1.6 seconds**—the **fastest acceleration of any coaster.**
  - Uses **compressed air launch technology**, making it one of the most intense launches ever built.

Future coasters may break the **150 mph barrier**, with new **magnetic propulsion systems** being developed to **launch trains even faster.**

The Longest Roller Coasters in the World

Some roller coasters focus less on **speed and height** and instead aim to provide the **longest ride possible**, making the experience last several minutes.

- **Steel Dragon 2000 (Nagashima Spa Land, Japan)**

  - **Track Length:** 8,133 feet (2,478 meters) – **longest coaster in the world.**
  - **Ride Duration:** Over **four minutes long**.
  - This **massive hyper coaster** was built to withstand **earthquakes** while delivering an experience packed with **big drops and high-speed airtime hills.**
- **The Beast (Kings Island, Ohio, USA)**

  - **Track Length:** 7,361 feet (2,243 meters).

- - The **longest wooden roller coaster in the world**, famous for its **twisting layout through the forest**.
- **Fury 325 (Carowinds, North Carolina, USA)**

  - **Track Length:** 6,602 feet (2,012 meters).
  - Considered one of the **best giga coasters ever built**, offering **huge drops and high-speed banked turns**.

Longer rides mean **more thrills per ride cycle**, and some parks aim to create **epic journeys through twists, turns, and drops that last several minutes**.

The Most Inversions Ever on a Ride

Some roller coasters focus on **spinning, flipping, and twisting riders upside down as many times as possible**. Over the years, amusement parks have battled to hold the record for **most inversions** on a single coaster.

- **The Smiler (Alton Towers, UK)**

  - **Inversions:** 14 – **world record for most inversions on a roller coaster**.
  - Features a mix of **corkscrews, loops, and heartline rolls**, flipping riders upside down repeatedly.
- **Colossus (Thorpe Park, UK)**

  - **Inversions:** 10 – The first coaster to reach **double-digit inversions**.
  - Inspired other high-inversion coasters around the world.
- **Blue Fire (Europa Park, Germany)**

- **Inversions:** 4 – While not a record-breaker, it features a **zero-G roll** that is considered one of the smoothest and most exciting inversions in the world.

Parks continue to **push the inversion record**, with new coasters being designed to create **even wilder flipping experiences**.

Strangest and Most Unique Roller Coasters

Not all record-breaking coasters are about **speed, height, or inversions**. Some break records simply by being **bizarre, creative, or completely different** from any other ride.

- **Eejanaika (Fuji-Q Highland, Japan)**

    - **Record:** Second-ever **4D coaster**, where seats rotate **360 degrees independently** as the train moves.
    - Riders **flip in every direction**, making each ride unpredictable.
- **Flying Dinosaur (Universal Studios Japan)**

    - **Record:** One of the **longest and tallest flying coasters** in the world.
    - Riders **hang face-down**, simulating the feeling of soaring through the sky.
- **Pipeline: The Surf Coaster (SeaWorld Orlando, USA)**

    - **Record:** First-ever **surf coaster**, where riders stand up on a moving platform that bounces slightly with the ride.
    - A completely **new style of roller coaster movement**.

Future roller coasters may continue to break records by **introducing entirely new ride systems** that offer **experiences never seen before**.

The Future of Record-Breaking Coasters

Roller coasters will **continue to evolve**, breaking even more records as parks **compete to build the biggest and best rides**. Some of the most exciting trends in coaster design include:

- **Coasters Over 500 Feet Tall** – Some parks are considering breaking the **strata coaster record** with rides taller than Kingda Ka.
- **Coasters That Break 150+ mph** – New launch technologies could create **even faster** coasters.
- **AI-Controlled Coasters** – Future rides could adjust speed and intensity **in real time** based on how riders react.
- **Completely Immersive Experiences** – Virtual reality and special effects will make coasters **more than just a ride—they'll be full experiences**.

Roller coasters have already reached **incredible heights, speeds, and levels of intensity**, but designers will **never stop pushing the limits**. The future promises even wilder rides that will redefine what's possible in amusement parks. The question is—**which record will be broken next?**

Chapter 16: The Future of Roller Coasters

Roller coasters have been thrilling riders for over a century, but they are far from reaching their peak. With each new generation, engineers and designers push the limits of **height, speed, technology, and experience** to make coasters more exciting, immersive, and efficient than ever before.

From virtual reality integration to artificial intelligence, the future of roller coasters is shaping up to be an era of **unparalleled thrills and innovation**. Could we see rides that **hover above the track, dive underwater, or even reach space?** Let's explore what's next for the world of roller coasters.

How Roller Coasters Are Evolving

As parks compete to offer the best rides, roller coasters continue to evolve in exciting ways.

Bigger, Faster, and More Thrilling Coasters

Parks are always looking to **break records** and **push the limits** with:

- **Taller rides** – The race for the **first 500-foot coaster** is on.
- **Faster speeds** – Launch coasters are reaching **150 mph and beyond**.
- **Wilder elements** – More inversions, steeper drops, and extreme airtime.

The focus isn't just on **numbers**—modern coasters also aim for **better ride experiences**, including:

- **Smoother, more intense movements** through advanced track shaping.

- **Multi-launch systems** that deliver unexpected bursts of speed.
- **Longer ride durations** to create unforgettable journeys.

Many of these improvements are thanks to **new construction techniques and materials**, allowing for bigger and more ambitious designs.

The Rise of Virtual Reality (VR) Coasters

One of the biggest trends in coaster technology has been the introduction of **VR-enhanced rides**. These rides combine a **real coaster track** with **virtual reality headsets** to create a fully immersive experience.

How VR Coasters Work

- Riders wear **VR headsets** that display a digitally created environment.
- The headset is **synced with the movement of the coaster**, making it feel like riders are flying through space, escaping a monster, or racing through a futuristic city.

Pros of VR Coasters

✔ Parks can **re-theme a ride without changing the physical coaster**.
✔ Allows for **completely different experiences** each time.
✔ Adds **extra storytelling** to a ride, making it more engaging.

Cons of VR Coasters

✘ **Longer wait times** due to the need for headset setup.

✘ Some riders experience **motion sickness**.

✘ Headsets require **constant maintenance and updates**.

While VR coasters have gained popularity, many parks have started **moving away from them** in favor of **physical theming and onboard special effects**, which provide **a more reliable and immersive experience without the drawbacks of VR technology**.

New Materials and Track Designs

In the past, roller coasters were built with either **wood or steel**, but modern coasters are now using **hybrid materials** and **new track designs** to improve the ride experience.

Hybrid Coasters: The Best of Both Worlds

- Hybrid coasters combine **wooden supports** with **steel track**, allowing for:
    - **Smoother rides** than traditional wooden coasters.
    - **Inversions and extreme elements** that wood coasters couldn't previously handle.
- Examples:
    - *Steel Vengeance* (Cedar Point) – An **RMC hybrid coaster** known for record-breaking airtime.
    - *Iron Gwazi* (Busch Gardens Tampa) – A conversion of a **classic wooden coaster into a steel hybrid monster**.

Stronger, Lighter Track Materials

- **Steel alloys and composite materials** are making roller coasters:

- More **durable** and **easier to maintain.**
- Capable of **crazier designs**, such as beyond-vertical drops and multi-directional tracks.
- Example: *Pantheon* (Busch Gardens Williamsburg) features a **flexible, lightweight steel track that enables multiple high-speed launches.**

These advancements allow for **bigger, faster, and more intense roller coasters that last longer and cost less to maintain.**

AI and Roller Coasters: The Future of "Smart Rides"

Artificial intelligence (AI) is becoming an important tool in the amusement park industry. It has the potential to **change how coasters operate**, making them more efficient, adaptive, and even customizable.

How AI Could Change Roller Coasters

1. **Smart Ride Systems That Adjust in Real-Time**

   - AI could **monitor weather, ride weight, and rider preferences** to adjust:
     - **Launch speeds** for a customized thrill level.
     - **Braking intensity** for a smoother or more forceful stop.
     - **Inversions or special elements** that activate based on rider choices.

2. **AI-Controlled Maintenance**

- AI could **detect mechanical issues before they happen**, making rides **safer and reducing downtime**.
- Some parks are already using **automated track monitoring systems** to scan for wear and tear.

3. **Adaptive Ride Experiences**

- Future rides may allow riders to **choose different routes** or **varying intensity levels** before boarding.
- Example: Imagine a **roller coaster with switchable track sections**, allowing for **multiple ride variations** in one coaster.

AI has the potential to make coasters **more interactive and personalized** while also improving **safety and efficiency**.

What the Future Holds

What will roller coasters look like in the next **50 years**? Engineers and designers are already experimenting with **mind-blowing concepts** that could redefine theme park thrills.

Predictions for the Future of Roller Coasters

1. **Underwater Roller Coasters**

- Coasters that **dive beneath lakes, oceans, or even ride through glass tunnels under water**.
- Special effects could make it **feel like riders are escaping sharks or traveling through an underwater city**.

2. **Space-Themed Coasters with Zero Gravity**

- Future coasters might **simulate weightlessness**, like an astronaut in space.
- Could involve **sudden floating moments** using controlled braking and acceleration techniques.

3. **Magnetic Hovering Coasters**

    - **Maglev (magnetic levitation) technology** could allow coasters to **float above the track with no wheels.**
    - This would create **a smoother, quieter, and more energy-efficient ride experience.**

4. **Self-Powered and Energy-Efficient Coasters**

    - Coasters that **generate their own energy** using **solar power or kinetic energy recovery systems.**
    - Future parks may aim for **zero-emission, eco-friendly ride technology.**

5. **Completely Immersive Story Coasters**

    - Rides that combine **trackless coaster systems with interactive storytelling**, making **every ride a unique adventure.**
    - Example: Imagine **choosing different paths** on a roller coaster, where each track change affects the story.

The possibilities are endless, and as **technology advances,** roller coasters will continue to evolve in **ways we can't even imagine today.**

The Next Chapter in Coaster History

Roller coasters are **only getting bigger, faster, and more advanced**. As new materials, AI, and ride systems emerge, coasters will offer **completely new ways to experience thrills**.

- **Hybrid coasters and lightweight materials** will allow for **wilder ride layouts.**
- **AI and adaptive ride systems** will make roller coasters **smarter and more personalized.**
- **Future innovations like magnetic hovering and energy-efficient coasters** could redefine how rides work.

With every new **record-breaking coaster**, the amusement park industry proves that **the future of roller coasters is just beginning**. Whether it's **underwater, in space, or breaking speed limits beyond what we thought possible**, the next generation of coasters will take us on **the wildest rides yet**.

Chapter 17: Famous Roller Coaster Designers

Behind every great roller coaster is a team of **engineers, designers, and visionaries** who bring these thrilling rides to life. While theme parks get most of the credit, the real magic comes from the **companies and individuals** who dream up, design, and build these incredible machines.

From the legendary **Werner Stengel**, who shaped modern coaster physics, to companies like **Intamin, Bolliger & Mabillard (B&M)**, and **Rocky Mountain Construction (RMC)**, these are the minds responsible for pushing the limits of roller coaster technology.

Who are the **greatest roller coaster designers** of all time, and how are new generations shaping the future of the industry? Let's take a ride through the **brains behind the thrills**.

Meet the Minds Behind the Rides

Building a roller coaster is **a mix of science, engineering, and artistry**. Some companies specialize in **record-breaking speed**, others in **smooth and comfortable rides**, and some in **theming and storytelling**.

Many of today's biggest coaster manufacturers have **signature styles**, meaning you can often tell **who built a coaster just by riding it**.

- **Some companies focus on breaking records** (height, speed, inversions).
- **Others focus on smooth, re-rideable experiences** that parkgoers love.
- **Some create immersive, story-driven rides** rather than just big thrills.

While coaster design is always evolving, a few **legendary names** have changed the industry forever.

The Genius of Werner Stengel

If you've ever ridden a **modern roller coaster**, you can thank **Werner Stengel**.

- **Who is Werner Stengel?**

    - A German engineer and coaster designer, born in 1936.
    - He worked closely with many of the biggest manufacturers, **shaping the way modern coasters are built**.
    - Known for his **innovative track shaping techniques**, which made coasters **safer, smoother, and more thrilling**.

- **His Greatest Innovations**

    - **The "Heartline Roll"** – Stengel was responsible for developing the concept that ensures **riders' bodies rotate naturally through inversions**, reducing discomfort and making loops feel effortless.
    - **The First Modern Vertical Loop** – His engineering led to **teardrop-shaped loops**, which allowed riders to go upside down **without excessive G-forces**.
    - **Mega and Giga Coasters** – He helped design some of the world's **tallest and fastest coasters**, like *Millennium Force* (Cedar Point).

Werner Stengel's work has influenced **almost every roller coaster built in the last 50 years,** making him one of the most **important figures in theme park history**.

Roller Coaster Companies That Changed the Industry

Several roller coaster manufacturers have **revolutionized theme parks** with their engineering breakthroughs. These companies continue to build **some of the most famous and thrilling rides ever created**.

Intamin – The Kings of Speed and Record-Breaking Coasters

- Intamin is known for **pushing the limits of speed and height**.
- Famous for:
    - *Kingda Ka* (Tallest coaster in the world at 456 feet).
    - *Formula Rossa* (Fastest coaster in the world at 149 mph).
    - *Millennium Force* (The first Giga coaster, 310 feet tall).
- Intamin coasters are **intense, fast, and full of innovation**.

Bolliger & Mabillard (B&M) – Masters of Smooth, Iconic Coasters

- B&M is **one of the most respected coaster manufacturers,** known for making **extremely smooth and comfortable rides**.
- Famous for:

- *Fury 325* (One of the best Giga coasters in the world).
- *The Incredible Hulk Coaster* (A powerful launch coaster at Universal).
- *Apollo's Chariot* (One of the first hyper coasters, focused on airtime).
- Their coasters are known for **buttery smooth rides and iconic looping elements**.

Rocky Mountain Construction (RMC) – The Hybrid Coaster Revolution

- RMC changed the industry by **combining wood and steel**, creating some of the wildest coasters ever built.
- Famous for:
  - *Steel Vengeance* (One of the most intense coasters ever made, at Cedar Point).
  - *Iron Gwazi* (A record-breaking hybrid coaster at Busch Gardens Tampa).
  - *Lightning Rod* (The first launched wooden coaster).
- RMC's coasters feature **crazy elements**, including **overbanked turns, extreme airtime, and unique inversions**.

These companies continue to push **roller coaster technology** forward, making each new ride **more exciting than the last**.

The Art of Theming and Storytelling

Some parks focus on **thrills**, while others focus on **immersion and storytelling**. The **best roller coasters combine both**, creating rides that are **exciting and unforgettable**.

How Disney Imagineers and Universal Studios Create Immersive Coaster Experiences

- **Disney's Approach**

    - Disney coasters focus on **story first**, using **animatronics, sound, and theming** to enhance the experience.
    - Examples:
        - *Space Mountain* (Darkness makes the ride feel faster than it actually is).
        - *Tron Lightcycle Run* (Motorcycle-style ride with neon futuristic theming).
        - *Expedition Everest* (An intense ride through the Himalayas, featuring a Yeti animatronic).
- **Universal's Approach**

    - Universal blends **high thrills with immersive storytelling**.
    - Examples:
        - *VelociCoaster* (Intense launches mixed with Jurassic World theming).
        - *Hagrid's Magical Creatures Motorbike Adventure* (A multi-launch coaster with animatronics and a surprise drop).
        - *Revenge of the Mummy* (A coaster mixed with special effects and fire).

While record-breaking speed is impressive, **themed coasters create an experience that feels like a journey rather than just a thrill ride.**

The Next Generation of Coaster Designers

As **theme parks and roller coasters continue to evolve**, new designers and engineers are stepping up to shape the future.

Who is Leading the Industry Today?

- Companies like **RMC, Intamin, B&M, and Vekoma** continue to innovate with new ride concepts.
- Engineers are now focusing on **AI-driven ride experiences, magnetic levitation coasters, and ultra-themed attractions**.

How Young Engineers Can Get Involved in Ride Design

If you're interested in designing roller coasters, consider:

- Studying **mechanical or structural engineering**.
- Learning about **physics and forces** that impact ride design.
- Gaining experience with **computer-aided design (CAD) software**.
- Interning or working with **theme parks or ride manufacturers**.

Becoming a coaster designer is a **dream job** for many theme park fans, and as technology advances, **there will be more opportunities than ever to create the next generation of thrill rides**.

The Legends Behind the Thrills

From **record-breaking giants to immersive story-driven rides**, roller coaster designers continue to shape the future of theme parks.

- **Werner Stengel** laid the foundation for modern roller coaster physics.
- **Companies like Intamin, B&M, and RMC continue to push the limits of height, speed, and inversions.**

- **Themed coasters at Disney and Universal prove that storytelling can be just as thrilling as speed.**
- **The next generation of engineers is already working on the future of roller coaster design.**

As technology advances, coaster designers will continue to create **bigger, better, and more mind-blowing rides**—ensuring that the **future of roller coasters is more exciting than ever before.**

Chapter 18: Roller Coasters in Movies and Pop Culture

Roller coasters aren't just a thrill-seeker's dream—they've also played a major role in **movies, television, music, video games, and advertising**. Whether they're used as thrilling action set pieces, symbols of excitement, or even metaphors for life's ups and downs, roller coasters have become a **cultural icon**.

From Hollywood blockbusters to theme park simulation games, let's explore how **roller coasters have influenced pop culture—and how pop culture has inspired real-life coasters.**

Famous Roller Coaster Scenes in Movies and TV Shows

Roller coasters have appeared in **countless films and television shows**, often as a setting for action, comedy, or suspense. Some of the most memorable coaster moments in entertainment include:

Coasters in Hollywood Films

- **Final Destination 3 (2006)** – One of the most famous roller coaster scenes in movie history, this horror film features a terrifying **coaster derailment sequence**. The scene made some people nervous about riding coasters, even though the movie is pure fiction.
- **Beverly Hills Cop III (1994)** – A high-speed action sequence takes place on a roller coaster at **Six Flags Magic Mountain**, featuring the real-life coaster *Revolution*.

- **Fear (1996)** – Features an intense scene on *The Roller Coaster* at **Playland Park (Canada)**.

Animated Shows Featuring Roller Coasters

Even in animation, roller coasters have played a big role in storytelling. Some famous examples include:

- **The Simpsons – "Bart the Daredevil" (1990)** – In one of the most famous episodes, Homer attempts to skateboard off a **massive canyon gap**, and the animation style mimics the extreme drops of a roller coaster.
- **SpongeBob SquarePants – "Roller Cowards" (2007)** – SpongeBob and Patrick visit **Glove World** to ride the extreme coaster *The Fiery Fist O' Pain*.
- **Phineas and Ferb – "Rollercoaster" (2007)** – The entire first episode revolves around the brothers building an **insanely over-the-top roller coaster** in their backyard.

Roller coasters are the perfect **visual symbol for excitement and fun**, which is why they frequently appear in both **live-action and animated storytelling**.

Roller Coasters in Video Games

Theme park and roller coaster simulation games have been **incredibly popular**, allowing players to **design their own coasters, manage amusement parks, and create thrilling experiences**.

RollerCoaster Tycoon (1999 – Present)

One of the most beloved video game franchises of all time, **RollerCoaster Tycoon** lets players:

- **Design custom roller coasters** from scratch, choosing tracks, loops, and drops.
- **Manage an amusement park**, balancing budgets and guest happiness.
- **Build extreme rides**, like vertical drops, high-speed launches, and even unsafe designs just for fun.

Other Roller Coaster-Themed Video Games

- **Planet Coaster (2016)** – A modern theme park simulation game, known for **advanced roller coaster customization**.
- **NoLimits Roller Coaster Simulator (2001-Present)** – A **realistic coaster simulation tool** used by actual ride designers to test layouts.
- **Thrillville (2006)** – A story-driven game where players **run a theme park and interact with guests**.

These games allow players to **experience the thrill of coaster design** from a creative and business perspective, further cementing roller coasters' place in entertainment.

Music and Songs About Roller Coasters

Roller coasters have long been used as **metaphors in music**, symbolizing excitement, love, and the ups and downs of life. Many famous songs have used roller coasters as inspiration:

Famous Songs Inspired by Roller Coasters

- **"Love Rollercoaster" – Ohio Players (1975)**
  - A funky hit about **the wild ride of love**, using roller coaster motion as a metaphor.
- **"Roller Coaster" – Bon Jovi (2016)**
  - A song about the **thrills and unpredictability of relationships**.

- **"Crazy Train" – Ozzy Osbourne (1980)**
  - While not directly about roller coasters, this rock anthem captures the **intensity and adrenaline of a high-speed ride.**

Why Roller Coasters Are Used as Metaphors in Pop Culture

- **Unpredictability** – Life, love, and emotions can feel like **a roller coaster ride**, full of highs and lows.
- **Excitement & Fear** – Roller coasters represent **thrill and adventure**, just like music often conveys strong emotions.

Music and pop culture often compare **life experiences to roller coasters**, reinforcing their status as a **symbol of excitement and intensity.**

Coasters That Became Legends

Some roller coasters have become **so famous that they are recognized even by people who have never ridden them**. These rides have appeared in **commercials, movies, books, and theme park advertisements**, becoming legendary in pop culture.

Iconic Roller Coasters in Pop Culture

- **Cyclone (Coney Island, New York)** – Featured in movies like *The Warriors (1979)*, this **classic wooden coaster** is one of the most famous in the world.
- **The Matterhorn Bobsleds (Disneyland)** – The first-ever **steel tubular coaster**, appearing in many Disney promotions.

- **Space Mountain (Disney Parks Worldwide)** – Known for its futuristic theme and **dark-ride thrills**, this ride has been featured in video games and movies.

These coasters are **more than just rides—they're cultural icons** that define amusement park history.

How Pop Culture Inspires Real-Life Coasters

It's not just that roller coasters appear in movies—sometimes, **movies inspire real-life roller coasters!** Many of today's most thrilling rides are based on **Hollywood films and franchises**.

Rides Based on Movies

- **Jurassic World VelociCoaster (Universal Orlando, 2021)**
    - A **high-speed, intense launch coaster** themed around **dinosaurs and the Jurassic World movies**.
- **The Incredible Hulk Coaster (Universal Orlando)**
    - A **powerful, high-speed looping coaster** based on Marvel's Hulk, with a **launch tunnel that simulates transformation into the Hulk**.
- **Harry Potter and the Escape from Gringotts (Universal Studios Florida)**
    - A mix of **dark ride storytelling and coaster elements**, bringing the world of Harry Potter to life.

How Theme Parks Partner with Hollywood

- **Movie studios work directly with coaster designers** to create rides that match film themes.
- Parks use **real props, set pieces, and even voice actors** from movies to enhance the ride experience.

- Some rides **help promote movies**, while others are created years later as permanent theme park attractions.

The partnership between **Hollywood and theme parks** has led to some of the most **innovative and immersive coaster experiences ever created**.

The Cultural Impact of Roller Coasters

Roller coasters are more than just amusement park rides—they've become **symbols of excitement, adventure, and unpredictability** in pop culture.

- **They appear in movies, TV shows, video games, and music,** shaping how we view thrills and excitement.
- **Some coasters have become legendary, appearing in advertisements, books, and popular culture for generations.**
- **Hollywood and theme parks continue to work together,** creating **blockbuster-inspired rides that bring movies to life.**

Whether you've seen them on the big screen, heard about them in songs, or played them in video games, roller coasters are **a major part of entertainment history**. Their presence in pop culture **ensures that the thrill of coasters will continue to capture imaginations for generations to come.**

Chapter 19: DIY Roller Coaster Science

Roller coasters may seem like massive, complex machines, but their basic principles can be tested and understood using **simple materials at home.** By building a **miniature roller coaster**, you can learn **firsthand how physics, energy, and motion work** in real rides.

Engineers use small-scale models to test new coaster designs before building **real full-sized roller coasters**, and you can do the same with **marbles, paper tubes, and household items.** This chapter will guide you through creating **your own mini roller coaster** and exploring the science behind the thrills.

Building Your Own Mini Coaster

You don't need expensive materials to create a working model of a roller coaster. You can build one using **items found around the house,** such as:

- **Cardboard tubes** (from paper towel or toilet paper rolls)
- **Straws or flexible plastic tracks**
- **Masking tape or glue**
- **A marble or small ball** (to act as the roller coaster train)
- **Books or boxes** (to create height for drops)

Steps to Build Your Mini Coaster

1. **Create the First Drop**

    ○ Start by **raising one end of your coaster track high** (this is like the **first hill on a real coaster**).

- Tape it to a stack of books or a chair to give it **enough height for the marble to roll down with speed**.
2. **Design the Track Layout**

   - Use tubes or strips of cardboard to create **curves, loops, and hills**.
   - Make sure there are no gaps where the marble could fall off.
3. **Test and Adjust**

   - Let the marble roll down and observe where it **slows down, stops, or falls off**.
   - Adjust the curves and slopes to make sure the marble **keeps moving** to the end.

This experiment mimics how real engineers test their coasters before building them in **full size**.

The Physics of a Homemade Coaster

Even on a small scale, your DIY coaster follows the same **laws of physics** that control real-life roller coasters.

How Height, Drops, and Loops Work

- **Potential Energy** – At the top of the first hill, your marble has **stored energy** from its height.
- **Kinetic Energy** – As the marble rolls down, its stored energy converts into **motion energy** (speed).
- **Gravity** – Pulls the marble downward, keeping it moving through dips and turns.
- **Friction** – Slows the marble down if the track is rough or too steep.

Why Hills and Curves Need the Right Shape

- If a hill is **too high**, the marble **loses speed and stops**.
- If a turn is **too sharp**, the marble may **fly off the track**.
- Engineers carefully design coasters so that trains have **just the right amount of speed** to complete the ride.

By testing different **heights, angles, and track shapes**, you can see how **real coaster physics** applies to your homemade ride!

Testing Speed and Energy

Once your mini coaster is working, you can **measure how fast the marble moves** and experiment with **different track designs**.

How to Measure Speed

- Use a **stopwatch** to time how long it takes for the marble to complete the track.
- Change the **height of the first drop** and compare the times.
- A taller first drop usually makes the marble **go faster** because it has **more energy at the start**.

Comparing Different Heights and Angles

- If you **increase the starting height**, does the marble go **faster or slower**?
- If you add a **loop**, does the marble have enough speed to make it through?
- Does the **type of material** (smooth vs. rough track) affect how far the marble goes?

These small experiments **mirror what real engineers do** when designing roller coasters.

Why Engineers Use Models Before Building Real Coasters

Before a full-size roller coaster is built, engineers create **small-scale models and computer simulations** to test:

- **How much speed the ride will need** to make it through loops and hills.
- **How forces like gravity and friction** affect the coaster's movement.
- **Where to place brakes and launch sections** to control ride pacing.

The Role of Prototypes and Small-Scale Testing

- Engineers often **build working models** using plastic tracks, mini motors, and small cars to test their designs.
- **Computer simulations** help predict how a ride will perform **before construction starts**.
- Testing allows them to make **adjustments** to avoid problems like **too much force, unsafe speeds, or uncomfortable turns**.

Just like **your DIY coaster**, real roller coasters go through a long process of **trial and error** before they are built full-size.

Fun Science Experiments at Home

Now that you understand the basics of roller coaster physics, here are some **fun challenges** to try with your DIY coaster.

Experiment 1: The Tallest First Drop

- Build **two different tracks**—one with a **low first hill** and one with a **tall first hill**.
- Which one makes the marble go **faster**?
- How does the height affect the marble's **final speed at the bottom**?

Experiment 2: The Perfect Loop

- Try creating a **loop** with a piece of flexible plastic or cardboard.
- What happens if the loop is **too big**? Does the marble have enough speed to complete it?
- How do you need to **adjust the first drop** to make the marble loop successfully?

Experiment 3: Longest Track Possible

- Challenge yourself to build the **longest, most exciting track** where the marble **never stops**.
- Add **curves, twists, and hills** to see how far you can keep it going!

These experiments **help you understand the same physics principles** used in real roller coaster design.

Engineering the Thrill at Any Scale

By building your own mini roller coaster, you've explored **how real coasters work** and how engineers use **physics, energy, and motion** to create thrilling rides.

- Roller coasters **convert potential energy into kinetic energy**, just like your marble track.
- Engineers **test their ideas with small models** before building full-size rides.

- You can **experiment at home** to better understand the science behind the thrills.

Whether it's a **backyard experiment** or a **full-sized theme park ride**, every roller coaster starts with a **simple idea and a love of physics**. Keep experimenting, designing, and challenging yourself—maybe one day, you'll create the next record-breaking roller coaster!

Chapter 20: The Ultimate Roller Coaster Bucket List

For true roller coaster fans, riding the world's most **legendary, record-breaking, and unique** coasters is the ultimate thrill-seeking adventure. But with **thousands of roller coasters around the world**, how do you know which ones deserve a spot on your **bucket list**?

This chapter will guide you through **must-ride coasters by category, planning a coaster road trip, and setting personal ride goals**. Whether you dream of tackling the **tallest, fastest, or most extreme rides**, this list will help you create your **own ultimate roller coaster challenge!**

What Makes a Coaster Bucket List-Worthy?

Not all roller coasters are created equal. Some rides become **bucket list legends** because they are:

- **World Record Holders** – Coasters that are **tallest, fastest, longest, or most extreme.**
- **One-of-a-Kind Experiences** – Unique rides that offer something **completely different from other coasters.**
- **Historical Icons** – Legendary coasters that have **stood the test of time.**
- **Themed Masterpieces** – Rides that **blend storytelling with thrills** in unforgettable ways.

A great bucket list coaster is one that **thrills, surprises, and leaves riders wanting more**—whether it's a **mind-blowing launch, a towering drop, or an innovative ride system.**

Bucket List Coasters by Category

No matter what kind of thrills you love, there's a bucket list coaster for you. Here are some of the most **famous and must-ride roller coasters in the world**, divided into key categories.

Tallest Coasters (For Those Who Love Heights)

- **Kingda Ka (Six Flags Great Adventure, USA)** – **Tallest coaster in the world (456 ft)**, with a breathtaking **straight-up launch**.
- **Red Force (Ferrari Land, Spain)** – The tallest **accelerator coaster in Europe**, reaching **367 feet** in seconds.

Fastest Coasters (For Speed Demons)

- **Formula Rossa (Ferrari World, UAE)** – The **fastest coaster on Earth** at **149 mph**! Riders even **wear goggles** to protect from the wind.
- **Do-Dodonpa (Fuji-Q Highland, Japan)** – Features the **fastest launch acceleration**, reaching **112 mph in just 1.6 seconds**.

Most Inversions (For Upside-Down Thrill Seekers)

- **The Smiler (Alton Towers, UK)** – Holds the **world record for most inversions (14 loops!)**.
- **Steel Curtain (Kennywood, USA)** – Has **9 inversions**, including the tallest inversion in the world at 197 feet.

Most Unique Coasters (For Riders Who Want Something Different)

- **Takabisha (Fuji-Q Highland, Japan)** – Features the **steepest drop in the world** at **121 degrees**!

- **X2 (Six Flags Magic Mountain, USA)** – A **4D coaster** where seats rotate 360 degrees as you ride.
- **Time Traveler (Silver Dollar City, USA)** – The **first spinning launch coaster**, with **crazy rotations and inversions**.

These are just a few of the most **unique and extreme rides** that **challenge the limits of coaster design.**

The Best Coasters for Every Thrill Level

Not all coasters are about **record-breaking intensity**—some are **perfect for beginners**, while others cater to **only the most fearless riders.**

Best Beginner-Friendly Coasters

For those new to roller coasters, these rides provide **thrills without overwhelming intensity:**

- **Big Thunder Mountain Railroad (Disney Parks)** – A great first coaster with **fun turns and mild drops**.
- **Seven Dwarfs Mine Train (Magic Kingdom, USA)** – A **smooth and gentle coaster** perfect for younger riders.
- **Verbolten (Busch Gardens Williamsburg, USA)** – A **mild launch coaster** with surprises, but no extreme drops.

Most Intense Coasters for Extreme Thrill-Seekers

For those who love **the most intense rides**, these are must-rides:

- **Skyrush (Hersheypark, USA)** – Known for its **extreme airtime** that lifts riders out of their seats.

- **Intimidator 305 (Kings Dominion, USA)** – A **giga coaster** with **intense G-forces that make some riders "gray out"**.
- **Eejanaika (Fuji-Q Highland, Japan)** – A **4D coaster that flips riders unpredictably throughout the ride.**

No matter your thrill level, there's a **bucket list coaster waiting for you.**

Planning a Coaster Road Trip

Visiting multiple amusement parks in one trip is the **best way to check off multiple bucket list coasters.** Here's how to plan a **perfect coaster road trip.**

Step 1: Pick Your Destination

- If you want **record-breakers**, visit **Cedar Point (Ohio), Six Flags Great Adventure (New Jersey), or Fuji-Q Highland (Japan).**
- If you want **theme park experiences**, visit **Disney, Universal, or Europa Park.**
- If you love **wooden classics**, visit **Kennywood (Pennsylvania) or Kings Island (Ohio).**

Step 2: Find the Best Time to Go

- Visit on **weekdays** to avoid long lines.
- Check park schedules—some parks **close on certain days** outside of summer.
- Consider **seasonal events**, like **Halloween haunt nights** for extra thrills.

Step 3: Maximize Your Rides

- Arrive **at park opening** to ride **the most popular coasters first**.
- Use **fast passes or single rider lines** to skip long waits.
- Stay **hydrated and take breaks** so you don't get coaster fatigue.

A well-planned coaster road trip can help you **check off multiple legendary rides in just a few days**.

How to Start Your Own Bucket List Challenge

If you want to **keep track of every roller coaster you ride**, here are some fun ways to do it:

Keeping Track of Coasters You've Ridden

- Use **Coaster-Count.com** or apps like **LogRide** to track every ride.
- Keep a **coaster journal** to rate and review each ride.
- Create a **scrapbook or photo album** of every major coaster trip.

Setting Ride Goals for the Future

- Try to **ride at least one new coaster every year**.
- Challenge yourself to visit a **new amusement park each season**.
- Aim to complete a **specific coaster challenge**, like:
    - Riding **all the B&M hypers**.
    - Visiting **every Disney park in the world**.
    - Riding the **top 10 fastest coasters**.

A roller coaster bucket list is a **lifelong adventure**—there's always another **record-breaker, legendary ride, or hidden gem** waiting to be conquered!

The Ride Never Ends

A roller coaster bucket list is about more than just **checking off rides**—it's about **experiencing new thrills, traveling to exciting places, and making lifelong memories.**

- Whether you dream of riding the **tallest coaster in the world, the fastest launch, or the most inversions**, there's always another challenge ahead.
- Planning a **coaster road trip** can help you **check off multiple bucket list rides** in one trip.
- Tracking your coaster rides and setting goals can **keep the excitement going for years to come.**

So, **what's next on your bucket list?** The world's greatest roller coasters are waiting—**buckle up and enjoy the ride!**

Printed in Dunstable, United Kingdom